# EL DESAYUNO SANO

### FRANCESC FOSSAS

*manuales* integral

**El desayuno sano**

Autor: Francesc J. Fossas
Diseño de cubierta: Josep Solà
Fotografía: Incolor
Compaginación: Pacmer, S. A. (Barcelona)

© octubre 1998, RBA Ediciones de Librerías, S. A.
   Pérez Galdós, 36 - 08012 Barcelona

Ref.: MI-14 / ISBN: 84-7901-378-8
Depósito Legal: B-37.802-98
Impreso por Liberdúplex (Barcelona)

# ÍNDICE

5

# INTRODUCCIÓN

Es una evidencia que existe una estrecha relación entre alimentación y salud. Un buen equilibrio nutricional es una condición *sine qua non* para mantener el estado de plenitud que deseamos. Pero la realidad se ha encargado de demostrar que no basta con disponer de alimentos suficientes para alcanzar este objetivo, y que nuestra capacidad de generar excedentes no es la solución definitiva frente a la amenaza de los desequilibrios nutricionales. Es necesario saber qué, cómo, cuánto y cuándo comer.

En un momento en que nuestra relación con el alimento está en crisis, se hace necesario seguir buscando (¿o encontrar de nuevo?), sin prisas, sin agobios, sin fundamentalismos ni dogmatismos, sin estereotipos, cuál es la mejor forma de conseguir aquello que necesitamos. Saber y sabor, he aquí dos conceptos unidos mucho más que por similitudes fonéticas.

Y no es una tarea fácil, pues la nutrición es una ciencia que aún cuenta con lagunas importantes, y las relaciones entre lo que comemos y el estado de salud en que nos encontramos no son tan sencillas, ni comer significa tan solo nutrirnos. Una constelación de variables hace que el avance sea lento. En este complejo panorama hay puntos más claros que otros: algunos aspectos gozan de un amplio consenso, mientras que otros muchos son altamente controvertidos y calurosamente debatidos. De entre los primeros, considerando nuestras tendencias y hábitos actuales y en el contexto de este manual, destacamos tres:

- La conveniencia de consumir más glúcidos complejos y menos grasas en general, grasas saturadas en particular.
- El interés en consumir más productos de origen vegetal y disminuir el exceso de alimentos de origen animal.
- Desayunar más y cenar menos.

Por diversas razones, el desayuno nos permite aprender muchas lecciones. Una de las más interesantes es la importancia que tiene el hecho de establecer unos ritmos alimentarios adecuados. Paralelamente, situado en un lugar de privilegio, del «des-ayuno» se espera que sepa detener con acierto el gasto de reservas corporales a que obliga el necesario descanso nocturno, y que además constituya una base adecuada para el equilibrio nutricional del día que empieza.

Actualmente, existe un amplio consenso sobre la mejor fórmula nutricional del desayuno: un aporte energético suficiente, una presencia generosa de glúcidos, moderada en proteínas y baja en grasas. Esta composición puede traducirse de una manera muy sencilla: en el desayuno deben estar presentes las frutas, los cereales y los alimentos lácteos, tres tipos de alimentos básicos que contribuyen, de forma decisiva, a satisfacer las necesidades de determinadas vitaminas y minerales fundamentales.

Apoyándose también en otras prestaciones de interés, como su rápida preparación, agradable sabor, fácil digestión y su economía, los expertos se han lanzado a promocionar este modelo de desayuno que encaja en el marco de lo que hoy se considera una forma saludable de alimentarse: la dieta mediterránea. De niños a ancianos, tanto hombres como mujeres, en la salud y en la enfermedad, todos, sin excepción, podemos beneficiarnos de un desayuno sano adaptado a cada circunstancia particular.

# EL AYUNO NOCTURNO

Si nuestras necesidades energéticas son constantes, ¿por qué no hay que comer continuamente? ¿Cuáles son nuestras necesidades nutricionales y cómo se abastecen? ¿Qué tipo de combustibles se almacenan en nuestro organismo? ¿Cuáles son las distintas especificidades de los diferentes tejidos en cuanto al tipo y la cantidad de combustibles consumidos?

El ayuno nocturno suscita éstas y otras muchas cuestiones; a partir de los conocimientos actuales sobre las mismas se establecen, hoy en día, las recomendaciones nutricionales y alimentarias para el desayuno.

## ¿DE QUÉ NOS NUTRIMOS POR LA NOCHE?

Diccionario en mano, por ayuno se entiende la abstención total o parcial de comer o beber. Afinando algo más, y desde un punto de vista nutricional, ayunar es, sobre todo, ingerir sólo agua.

El necesario descanso diario de nuestro organismo conlleva una ausencia de ingesta alimentaria. Entre 10 y 12 horas sin comer suele ser el ayuno máximo al que sometemos a nuestro organismo cotidianamente. La importancia del «des-ayuno» es que, como literalmente indica el término, es el acto alimentario con el que interrumpimos el ayuno.

El interés de los alimentos reside, desde un punto de vista nutricional, en su contenido en nutrientes, cuyas necesidades, a su vez, están determinadas por el particular funcionamiento de nuestro metabolismo. Las necesidades energéticas de nuestras células son constantes; no obstante, ello no nos obliga a consumir alimentos con que obtener los combustibles necesarios de forma continua. La explicación reside en que nuestro organismo es capaz de almacenar determinada cantidad de sustratos energéticos que moviliza entre los períodos de ingesta. Estas reservas energéticas son las que permiten, por ejemplo, que, asumiendo un gasto energético de 1 Cal / kg· h, un hombre de 70 kg consuma durante 8 horas de sueño 560 Calorías (Cal) sin tener necesidad de comer. De hecho, como es sabido, un ayuno puede prolongarse durante bastantes días.

Las reservas energéticas corporales están constituidas fundamentalmente por:

- El glucógeno: un glúcido complejo, constituido básicamente por muchas moléculas de glucosa, que se almacena de forma importante en el hígado y los músculos.
- Las grasas: que se almacenan en grandes cantidades en el tejido adiposo y que, con diferencia, representan la reserva energética cuantitativamente más importante del organismo (tabla 1).

En relación con nuestra composición corporal, una característica muy importante que debe señalarse es que, a pesar de figurar entre los componentes

## TABLA 1. RESERVAS ENERGÉTICAS DEL ORGANISMO EN UN HOMBRE ADULTO

| Nutriente | Cantidad | Localización |
|---|---|---|
| Triglicéridos (grasas) | 9.000 g | tejido adiposo |
| Glucógeno | 90 g | hígado |
| Glucógeno | 350 g | músculos |

Nota: la reserva de grasas en una mujer adulta de peso normal es aproximadamente el 25 % del total de su peso, lo que para una mujer de 55 kg representaría alrededor de 14.000 g.

mayoritarios de nuestro cuerpo, el agua (alrededor del 60 % del peso corporal) y las proteínas (el 17 % y el 13 % para hombres y mujeres, respectivamente) no constituyen reserva alguna; dicho de otra forma: cualquier desajuste por defecto entre sus aportes y gastos provocará rápidamente un balance negativo de las mismas.

Dado que las grasas no pueden convertirse en glúcidos y que la glucosa del glucógeno muscular no puede salir de los músculos, la única posibilidad metabólica que le queda al organismo para mantener unos niveles de glucosa constantes, cuando no hay ingesta, es la reserva de glucógeno del hígado. Pero, como puede observarse en la tabla 1, esta reserva es cuantitativamente pequeña. Aun así, este mecanismo es absolutamente esencial para mantener una de las constantes más fundamentales de nuestra economía orgánica: la glucemia (nivel de glucosa en la sangre).

Nuestra vida depende del mantenimiento de un nivel de glucemia suficiente y ello es debido, en gran parte, a que la glucosa representa el sustrato más importante para el metabolismo energético del cerebro. El cerebro consume alrededor de 120 g de glucosa diarios, es decir, unos 5 g/h, lo que representa alrededor de un 25 % del consumo energético total en reposo.

Con nuestros ritmos alimentarios habituales, sólo dos mecanismos intervienen de forma importante en el mantenimiento constante de la glucemia dentro de rangos normales:

- La ingesta de alimentos: entrada de glucosa a través del tubo digestivo.
- Glucogenólisis hepática: liberación de glucosa a la circulación procedente del glucógeno del hígado.

Estos dos mecanismos ejemplifican las alternativas básicas con las que se encuentra nuestro metabolismo energético diariamente: fase de alimentación y fase de hambre. Durante el ayuno nocturno, las reservas hepáticas de glucógeno resultan fundamentales para mantener una glucemia adecuada, y por esta razón se hallan disminuidas por la mañana. Puesto que otros tejidos, excepto el cerebro y las células glucógeno-dependientes, pueden utilizar las grasas como combustible, una forma que tiene el organismo de economizar las escasas reservas glucídicas que posee es movilizar las grasas almacenadas. Esto es lo que ocurre durante el ayuno nocturno: el abastecimiento energético de nuestras células se caracteriza por la liberación de la glucosa hepática y la movilización de grasas del tejido adiposo.

Por ello, cuando no hay desayuno y la falta de aporte de nutrientes se prolonga, pueden aparecer dos nuevos fenómenos adaptativos que, no obstante, van a presentar facturas elevadas:

- El aumento de la velocidad de movilización de las grasas puede conducir a la síntesis de cuerpos cetónicos. Los cuerpos cetónicos son un combustible que elabora el hígado a partir de los ácidos grasos y pueden ser utilizados por el cerebro como alternativa a la glucosa, lo cual disminuye la necesidad de la misma. Sin embargo, concentraciones elevadas de compuestos cetónicos pueden plantear problemas metabólicos.
- Las proteínas musculares, de las que, recordémoslo, no hay reservas, pueden ser utilizadas como materia prima para la obtención de nueva glucosa. El precio es caro puesto que se pierden estructuras corporales.

Así pues, y a modo de resumen, la situación planteada es la siguiente: el cerebro, cuyo único combustible en el ayuno temprano sigue siendo la glucosa, necesita proveerse constantemente de este combustible; ello, a su vez, depende de unos niveles adecuados de glucosa en la sangre, niveles que, en esta situación, dependen única y exclusivamente de las limitadas reservas de glucógeno del hígado.

Todo ello nos conduce de forma inevitable a un nuevo interrogante.

## ¿QUÉ NOS PIDE EL CUERPO POR LA MAÑANA?

Dado el panorama metabólico expuesto, resulta evidente que lo que nos pide el cuerpo por la mañana es glucosa. La ingestión de alimentos que nos proporcionen glucosa invertirá el rumbo de los acontecimientos. Esta glucosa absorbida estimulará la secreción de insulina, la gran hormona del almacenamiento, que preside la regulación metabólica durante la fase de alimentación.

La insulina, segregada por el páncreas, ejerce numerosos efectos metabólicos encaminados hacia una misma dirección: la formación de reservas energéticas y la detención de los procesos de movilización; así, aumenta el transporte de glucosa en los tejidos muscular y adiposo, estimula la formación de glucógeno al tiempo que inhibe su utilización, evita la movilización de las grasas del tejido adiposo y estimula su síntesis. Además, sólo la glucosa de la dieta permitirá restablecer los niveles de glucógeno hepático y preparar al organismo para hacer frente a nuevos períodos de hambre.

Así pues, la combinación de estos dos factores, ingesta de glúcidos y aumento de la liberación de insulina, permitirá la transición metabólica desde el uso de las propias reservas a la utilización y almacenamiento de los nutrientes ingeridos.

El desayuno y la indicación específica de la ingesta de glúcidos que lo acompaña demuestran, una vez más, que la importancia del aporte energético no sólo descansa en la cantidad de calorías ingeridas, sino también en el tipo de combustibles que las proporcionan y en el ritmo de las ingestas de los mismos, es decir, tanto en aspectos cuantitativos como cualitativos. Cualquier desequilibrio de alguno de estos factores puede alterar nuestra compleja economía.

Pero, además de su aspecto eminentemente fisiológico, el desayuno, al igual que otras ingestas alimentarias, también podrá provocar efectos psicológicos ligados, en parte, a la secreción de hormonas gastrointestinales, como, por ejemplo, la sensación de bienestar que se experimenta tras la toma de alimento.

Puesto que el nutriente más importante que hay que ingerir por la mañana es la glucosa, cabe preguntarse: ¿dónde se halla esta sustancia? Los principales alimentos básicos que, en distintas presentaciones, acaban proporcionando la mayor parte de la glucosa que el cuerpo necesita son los cereales, las legumbres, las patatas y la fruta. Algunos de ellos serán los elegidos para empezar el día.

# HÁBITOS Y TENDENCIAS: DESAYUNAMOS MAL

En la larga lista de errores alimentarios colectivos figura el de efectuar un mal desayuno. Con los hábitos y tendencias actuales se cometen algunos errores de bulto que antes o después acaban por pasar factura.

La práctica de desayunar mal no responde a un hecho puntual, sino que se engloba en un marco mucho más amplio, en el que factores tales como un conocimiento escaso de nuestras necesidades nutricionales, un mal conocimiento de la composición de los alimentos y el seguimiento de horarios no siempre acordes con nuestra salud, desempeñan un papel destacado.

## ALGUNOS ERRORES DE BULTO

Uno de los principales motivos para el estudio de la importancia del desayuno en el equilibrio nutricional es que, en su práctica habitual, se detectan gran número de errores importantes que alteran la propia ingesta de alimentos y repercuten en nuestro equilibrio nutricional global. Los principales errores de bulto atribuibles a nuestro desayuno actual es que éste resulta:

**Escaso**

El porcentaje de energía aportado por nuestro desayuno no alcanza las cotas recomendadas por los expertos. Desayunar poco y mal no puede compensarse con la ingesta a lo largo de todo el día de las calorías necesarias, ya que con ello sólo provocaremos que se produzcan desequilibrios cualitativos entre los distintos responsables de estos aportes. De lo dicho se desprende que una distribución adecuada de las ingestas resulta fundamental para el equilibrio alimentario.

**Pobre en frutas**

El consumo diario de frutas y hortalizas se considera hoy como una de las estrategias que es necesario adoptar para la prevención de algunos de los problemas de salud más importantes que padecemos. Por poner sólo un ejemplo, la recomendación de comer con frecuencia fruta es una de las medidas que figuran en el Código Europeo contra el Cáncer. El desayuno es, como veremos, el momento ideal para una de las dos raciones de fruta diarias que como mínimo deberíamos tomar.

**Excesivo en grasas**

Uno de los principales errores de nuestra dieta actual es la ingesta excesiva de grasas a expensas de glúcidos complejos (almidón). Y es que el aumento del poder adquisitivo permite consumir más alimentos grasos y menos glucídicos, ya que estos últimos suelen rechazarse con el pretexto de que son alimentos de «pobres» (en el fondo, el factor condicionante de estos cambios nutricionales es la sustitución de los alimentos de origen vegetal por alimentos de origen animal).

En especial interesa el exceso de un tipo de grasas, las saturadas, cuyo consumo excesivo se relaciona con el aumento del nivel de colesterol plasmático. Las grasas saturadas son las que predominan, a excepción del pescado, en los alimentos de origen animal. Pero, ligada a la nueva oferta de la industria alimentaria, una nueva fuente de grasas saturadas se revela como extraordinariamente importante. Se trata de los productos de bollería que utilizan este tipo de grasas en su elaboración, ya sea prodecentes directamente de fuentes animales, de fuentes vegetales con elevado índice de saturación, o bien obtenidas a partir de la hidrogenación (saturación) de grasas insaturadas de origen vegetal.

Esto es particularmente importante porque muchos de estos productos se consumen en el desayuno actual; lo cual, aun siendo de gran relevancia para todos los colectivos, adquiere un énfasis especial en el mundo infantil.

## Excesivo en azúcar

El azúcar (sacarosa) es un alimento polémico. Su omnipresencia se debe no sólo a su uso como edulcorante, sino a su empleo masivo en múltiples productos de elaboración industrial. En el desayuno suele utilizarse, a veces en grandes cantidades, de distintas formas.

Un desayuno en el que se consuman cuatro cucharadas pequeñas (de las llamadas de café) de azúcar, y un producto cereal azucarado y/o alimentos como mermeladas o chocolate, puede proporcionar entre 30 y 40 g de azúcar. ¡Y el día no ha hecho más que empezar!

Esto quiere decir que el consumo de un alimento desprovisto de cualquier otra cosa que no sea sacarosa, es decir, una «caloría vacía», proporcionará el 20 % del Valor Calórico Total (VCT) de una dieta de 2.000 Calorías. Esto es, sin ningún género de dudas, demasiado azúcar.

## Pobre en fibra

Ni las grasas ni el azúcar, cuya presencia, como acabamos de comentar, es excesiva en el desayuno habitual actual, contienen fibra. Con lo que, a medida que aumenta la presencia de aquéllos en la dieta, disminuye la posibilidad de obtener este tipo de compuestos no digeribles por nuestro tubo digestivo. Actualmente, se recomienda una ingesta de entre 30 y 35 g diarios de fibra.

El interés actual por la fibra se centra en sus efectos sobre el tiempo de tránsito intestinal, y también en sus posibles efectos benéficos sobre el metabolismo de glúcidos y colesterol.

## Excesivo en café

El café contiene cafeína. Las consecuencias de la ingesta de cafeína sobre la salud han estado siempre rodeadas de polémica. La conveniencia o no de su consumo debe juzgarse, como en tantos otros casos en materia alimentaria, desde la relación beneficios/riesgos.

En el lado de los beneficios, y teniendo en cuenta que el café tiene un valor nutricional nulo, sus únicos efectos positivos pueden ser el placer de degustarlo, los posibles efectos esperados de la cafeína y la convivencia que suele acompañar a su consumo; por el otro lado, el sabor amargo despierta las sospechas sobre el posible riesgo de su ingestión. Una cuestión que parece admitida es que estos riesgos dependen tanto de la cantidad ingerida como de las distintas susceptibilidades individuales. La cafeína se considera una sustancia psicoactiva (capaz de producir efectos psicológicos) que, con un consumo de entre 20 y 200 mg diarios, suele producir efectos de alerta, energía y bienestar, mientras que de 200 a 800 mg produce nerviosismo, ansiedad y temblor, en especial si no se toma habitualmente.

Algunos estudios señalan que la dependencia física se alcanza cuando se consumen entre 400 y 600 mg de cafeína diarios durante más de 1-2 semanas, y se observa dolor de cabeza, fatiga, letargia y ansiedad tras 12-24 horas de no ingerirla. Probablemente, uno de los principales problemas ligados a su consumo se relacione con aquellas situaciones en las que el café resulta un elemento indispensable para «arrancar». Toda una evidencia de que el verdadero motor no se halla en buenas condiciones.

Por otro lado, si bien la cafeína puede inducir un aumento de la actividad del sistema nervioso simpático, lo que constituye una posible causa de aumento de la presión arterial, importantes revisiones sobre el tema concluyen que, en personas sanas, el consumo moderado de café no modifica la función cardíaca ni la tensión arterial, al tiempo que su acción hipercolesterolémica no está todavía probada y, en caso de existir, sería muy débil.

En definitiva, en el estado actual de las cosas, los expertos concluyen que una persona sana puede tomar dos o tres cafés diarios no muy cargados, es decir, unos 200 mg de cafeína al día.

**Hábitos inadecuados**

Lo que parece verdaderamente nefasto en relación a los hábitos inadecuados en el desayuno es que comienzan desde muy temprano. Son muchos los niños que desayunan poco y mal. Pero, estudios recientes han mostrado que, lejos de corregirse, estos defectos empeoran con la edad. Así, datos recientemente publicados indican que durante la adolescencia se desayuna peor que en la infancia. Este efecto dominó negativo no parece detenerse al llegar a la madurez.

De ello se deduce que la práctica de un mal desayuno acompaña a muchas personas a lo largo de todo su ciclo vital.

## ¿QUÉ OFRECE EL «DESAYUNO DE CAFETERÍA»?

Las características nutricionales del desayuno actual quedan totalmente integradas en lo que convenimos en llamar «desayuno de cafetería». Y es que, en efecto, tras una ojeada a las ofertas de las múltiples cafeterías que nos ofrecen sus servicios, podemos elaborar un modelo de denominador común: café con leche y una pasta. Esta fórmula tan recurrida respeta, uno por uno, todos los errores de bulto anteriormente señalados.

Existen argumentos bastante contundentes en contra del desayuno lejos del hogar: desayunar fuera de casa aumenta el riesgo de que éste sea insuficiente y desequilibrado.

Si, como ocurre a menudo, la utilización de la fórmula se debe más a límites de elección que a verdadero goce por ella, obtendremos un beneficio realizando algunas modificaciones que, dentro de las condiciones establecidas, la pueden mejorar.

Tomar una pieza de fruta o un zumo natural antes de salir de casa cambia algunos aspectos negativos del desayuno actual (las oportunidades de tomar un buen zumo natural en los establecimientos de restauración son desgraciadamente escasas; la relación calidad/precio resulta raramente satisfactoria). Por su parte, la pasta puede ser sustituida por un bocadillo de queso, una ración de coca o alguna otra preparación de la que sepamos que tiene un bajo contenido en grasa; con ello aumentaremos el consumo de glúcidos y disminuiremos el de grasa saturada. El café con leche puede modificarse: cuanta más leche y menos café, mejor. También puede sustituirse por dos yogures naturales.

## LA FACTURA DE UN MAL COMIENZO

¿Cuáles son las consecuencias de desayunar mal?, o hablando en positivo, ¿por qué es tan importante desayunar bien?

La respuesta incluye tanto las esferas fisiológicas como psicológicas, tanto las consecuencias tempranas como las tardías. En este sentido, hay una premisa que resulta muy importante: los desequilibrios nutricionales no ejercen siempre un efecto inmediato sobre la salud, lo que sirve para demostrarnos nuevamente la notable capacidad de adaptación del organismo.

Las principales patologías que padece nuestro mundo civilizado, y en las que la nutrición desempeña una función importante (muy a menudo clave), necesitan de errores continuados para desarrollarse hasta sus etapas clínicas. Un exceso de peso no se «fabrica» en un día, ni en una semana, como tampoco se tapona una arteria o se debilitan los huesos al cabo de un mes de desórdenes alimentarios.

No obstante, las consecuencias de un mal desayuno pueden tener también efectos inmediatos sobre aquellos colectivos cuyo equilibrio nutricional es, por diferentes razones, más frágil.

## Sobre el equilibrio alimentario global

Por su «posición estratégica», el desayuno tiene una importancia clave en el equilibrio nutricional y alimentario: si nos saltamos esta primera ingesta, o resulta insuficiente en cuanto a alimentos básicos, va a ser muy difícil obtener todo el aporte energético que necesitamos con el resto de tomas. En este sentido, y a título de ejemplo, existen datos que indican que los niños que no desayunan no alcanzan ni las 2/3 partes de los aportes recomendados en micronutrientes.

Por otro lado, si el desayuno está presidido por ingestas importantes de grasas y azúcar, no sólo no mejorará el aporte de micronutrientes, sino que, además, será más que probable que acabemos ingiriendo cantidades excesivas de nutrientes energéticos. Con nuestros hábitos actuales, ambas cosas suelen ser demasiado frecuentes. Deficiencias y excesos constituyen el panorama nutricional en que nos movemos, algo que un buen desayuno puede contribuir a solventar.

## Sobre el peso corporal

Sea por una ingesta excesiva de alimentos calóricos, por un «picoteo» descontrolado como consecuencia de una toma insuficiente, o por una concentración excesiva de las tomas restantes cuando el desayuno ha sido escaso o nulo, un desayuno inadecuado puede repercutir desfavorablemente sobre el peso corporal.

Son las cenas copiosas las que más se relacionan con el aumento de peso, pues parece que el organismo fabrica más fácilmente reservas durante la noche. Un buen desayuno resulta fundamental para un reparto correcto de las tomas alimentarias a lo largo de la jornada.

## Sobre la salud cardiovascular

Hoy nuestros hábitos alimentarios nos conducen a una ingesta excesiva de grasas saturadas. Es evidente que, de entre los alimentos que las contienen, es prioritario eliminar aquéllos menos fundamentales. En esta situación, y con referencia a los hábitos de desayuno, debemos situar como gran protagonista a la bollería, cuyo contenido en grasas saturadas suele ser notable.

Los niños son uno de los grandes colectivos de consumo, si no el mayor, de este tipo de productos. Los expertos señalan que el excesivo consumo de productos de bollería podría ser la causa de que los niveles de colesterol de los niños españoles sea en la actualidad alarmantemente elevado, y muestran por ello su preocupación, no sólo por el presente sino también por lo que sucederá dentro de 20 o 30 años, cuando estos niños (y más los niños que las niñas), ya adultos, puedan padecer las consecuencias de tales errores.

En la actualidad se considera que el proceso arteriosclerótico se inicia a edad temprana. En el marco de la XIII Semana del Corazón, organizada por la Fundación Española del Corazón en octubre de 1997, se señaló que «los hábitos de un consumo excesivo de sal y grasas se adquieren en la infancia, y esas grasas son la causa de la formación de placas de ateroma en las arterias». El impacto de estos hechos sobre la salud pública es evidente, máxime si se considera que, hoy en día, las enfermedades cardiovasculares son la principal causa de mortalidad en España.

Otras fuentes importantes de grasas saturadas en pediatría son la mantequilla, un consumo excesivo de leche y sus derivados, tales como leches fermentadas y quesos, y las hamburguesas.

## Sobre la salud de los huesos

Los huesos son un tejido dinámico que se está reconstruyendo constantemente. Entre los nutrientes fundamentales que lo constituyen, el más precario en la dieta de nuestro medio suele ser el calcio. El equilibrio cálcico pasa por una ingesta suficiente de lácteos, la mejor fuente no sólo cuantitativa, sino también cualitativa de este elemento.

Para garantizar un buen estado nutricional cálcico se recomienda, a cualquier edad, una adecuada ingesta diaria de alimentos ricos en calcio. Hoy se sabe que los problemas óseos, que se presentan especialmente en la mujer posmenopáusica y en los ancianos de ambos sexos, pueden ser el fruto de una ingesta insuficiente de calcio en las primeras décadas de la vida, en las que se forma más hueso del que se destruye y donde, en definitiva, se fijará el capital óseo del que dispondrá posteriormente el individuo.

## Sobre el rendimiento físico e intelectual

Si bien en relación con la manifestación de una patología crónica hay que buscar los factores que contribuyen a su aparición, no ocurre lo mismo con otros aspectos de nuestras potencialidades. Éste es el caso del rendimiento físico e intelectual, máxime en aquellos colectivos con un equilibrio nutricional más frágil, como, por ejemplo, en los niños.

Recordemos que las funciones cerebrales dependen del aporte energético, y que, en condiciones normales el único combustible para las neuronas es la glucosa. En consecuencia, y en relación con el rendimiento intelectual, la máxima prioridad es conseguir un consumo suficiente de este glúcido.

Se ha señalado que los niños en situación de estrés metabólico, debido al ayuno, tienen una memoria alterada y un nivel de atención inferior, lo que les impide hacer una buena selección de la información; asimismo se ha demostrado que la glucosa ejerce un papel decisivo en el funcionamiento de la memoria. También se ha indicado que las facultades de elocución y la creatividad se ven particularmente afectadas por la ausencia del desayuno, y que la capacidad de aprender tiene que ver con el tiempo que hace que se ha comido. En definitiva, de los resultados de un conjunto de importantes trabajos se desprende que el desayuno mejora las actividades cognitivas durante el curso de la mañana, y que es muy importante tomarlo a diario antes de ir a la escuela. Estos beneficios sobre la capacidad intelectual han sido demostrados también en adultos jóvenes y ancianos.

También se ha observado un mejor humor en aquellos niños que desayunan, lo que podría explicarse por el confort psicosocial experimentado por los sujetos, que se tornan más amistosos y extravertidos.

El niño sano es naturalmente activo. Esta actividad se expresa mediante el movimiento, que depende del mecanismo de contracción muscular, el cual, a su vez, necesita de un aporte de energía. El combustible principal del músculo es la glucosa, que puede proceder tanto del glucógeno almacena-do como de la glucosa sanguínea. Una actividad física intensa, como la que puede darse en una sesión matinal de gimnasia, puede comprometer aún más un metabolismo pobre en glucosa; de ello pueden resentirse tanto la propia actividad física como el rendimiento en las aulas. Este interés especial en el consumo de glucosa ligado a la actividad física se hace extensible a cualquier franja de edad.

# EL MEJOR DESAYUNO

Acabamos de ver cuáles son las principales consecuencias negativas de un mal desayuno. ¿Cuál es entonces la alternativa?, ¿qué se considera en la actualidad un buen desayuno?, ¿qué nutrientes y qué alimentos deben componerlo? Hoy en día, la respuesta a estos interrogantes es bastante clara y unánime.

## UN BUEN DESAYUNO COMIENZA CON UNA BUENA CENA

Hemos visto que nuestro organismo se nutre mediante ciclos de alimentación-hambre. Una de las cuestiones básicas que surgen al plantearnos el equilibrio nutricional es: ¿cuántas veces debemos comer?, o lo que es lo mismo, ¿qué ritmos alimentarios son los más adecuados?

Ciertamente no existe un único modelo al respecto. En la inmensa mayoría de los casos, lo más adecuado es repartir el volumen total de alimentos ingeridos entre tres y seis tomas. Un número menor somete al organismo a períodos de hambre relativamente largos y obliga a ingerir volúmenes demasiado elevados en cada una de las tomas; si es mayor, deja poco tiempo para la digestión de la toma anterior.

Convencionalmente aceptamos que son tres las ingestas de comida principales: el desayuno, la comida del mediodía y la cena. Una toma a media mañana y la merienda suelen ser también habituales, y en determinados colectivos necesarias, mientras que en algunos casos se instaura una ingesta adicional antes de ir a la cama.

Los ritmos alimentarios están más interrelacionados de lo que pueda parecer. La alteración de una ingesta puede desencadenar un efecto en cascada que afecte a todas las demás. Así, en el caso que nos ocupa, una cena tardía y/o copiosa puede alterar, no sólo el sueño, sino también el desayuno.

Lo ideal sería: cena temprana y no excesivamente pesada ni abundante. ¡Lástima que lo ideal se aleje, a veces, tanto de lo real! Lo cierto es que muchos de los constreñimientos ambientales que tanto condicionan nuestro modelo alimentario actual son de difícil modificación, y tenemos que atenernos a esa realidad.

Con todo, haríamos bien si no ingiriésemos cantidades excesivas de comida y moderáramos el aporte de grasas en ese momento del día.


## ¿QUÉ NOS RECOMIENDAN LOS EXPERTOS?

Junto con numerosas divergencias existen también proposiciones que gozan de un alto grado de consenso. Éste es el caso del desayuno, sobre el que existe un acuerdo general acerca de su importancia, y una notable unanimidad acerca de cuál debe ser su composición.

### Energía

El equilibrio energético es lo primero que debe respetar una dieta equilibrada. Sólo un aporte de calorías equivalente al gasto permitirá mantener el peso corporal. Si tomamos más calorías de las que gastamos, se acumularán en forma de grasa en el organismo y aumentaremos de peso. Si, por el contrario, la ingesta es menor al gasto, perderemos peso: éste es el principio de las dietas hipocalóricas.

Así pues, el gran interrogante que se plantea a menudo acerca de cuántas calorías necesitamos diariamente, se resuelve de una forma relativamente sencilla: las que nos permitan mantener un peso estable.

Los ritmos alimentarios determinan en qué forma vamos a incorporar la energía que necesitamos. Ya se ha señalado que se considera un mínimo de tres ingestas diarias. En este contexto, al desayuno se le suele hacer responsable de un 25 % del total. Es decir, en una dieta de 2.200 Cal, 550 se incorporarán por la mañana.

### Glúcidos

Los glúcidos son, desde el punto de vista cuantitativo, el nutriente más importante de la dieta. Una comida con pocos glúcidos obligará, inevitablemente, a ingerir demasiadas grasas y/o proteínas para alcanzar las necesidades energéticas del individuo. En la actualidad se recomienda que los glúcidos nos aporten entre el 50 y el 60 % del total de Calorías. El siguiente ejemplo clarificará estas cifras:

$$\text{VCT: 2.200 Cal} \xrightarrow{60\%} \text{1.320 Cal} \xrightarrow{\div 4\ \text{Cal/g}} \text{330 g}$$

Es decir, en una dieta cuyo valor calórico total (VCT) sean 2.200 Cal, el 60 % representan 1.320 Cal. El paso de calorías a gramos es posible admitiendo que los glúcidos proporcionan 4 calorías por cada gramo (n° de Atwater). En total, la dieta debe incorporar 330 g de glúcidos.

Tras resolver el aspecto cuantitativo de los glúcidos, debe abordarse el cualitativo. El glúcido mayoritario debe ser el almidón, que es la forma en que los vegetales almacenan su glucosa, es decir, el equivalente a nuestro glucógeno. La limitación de la ingesta de glúcidos se centra fundamentalmente en la toma de azúcares.

Los azúcares son un tipo de glúcidos que se caracterizan por su sabor dulce y por ser solubles en agua; los azúcares más importantes en nuestra alimentación habitual son:

- La sacarosa: compuesta de glucosa y fructosa; es lo que habitualmente llamamos «azúcar». Pero, además de encontrarse en el azucarero y en gran cantidad de productos comestibles, la sacarosa se encuentra de forma natural en las frutas, donde se encuentran también la fructosa y la glucosa libres.
- La lactosa: formada de la unión de glucosa y galactosa; la lactosa es un azúcar propio de los alimentos lácteos. La leche y las leches fermentadas son sus fuentes. El queso prácticamente no la contiene.

Así pues, la segunda gran recomendación actual acerca de los glúcidos es de orden cualitativo y propone que los azúcares no aporten más del 10 % del VCT. Retomando el ejemplo anterior:

$$\text{VCT: 2.200 Cal} \xrightarrow{10\,\%} 220 \text{ Cal} \xrightarrow{\div\,4\,\text{Cal/g}} 55 \text{ g de azúcares}$$

Resumiendo, sabemos que una dieta de 2.200 Cal, de las que el 60 % son glúcidos, deberá contener 330 g de este tipo de nutriente, de los cuales 275 g (330 - 55) serán almidón y 55 g azúcares.

Todo ello tiene consecuencias prácticas muy directas:

- La principal fuente de glúcidos de la dieta serán los alimentos ricos en almidón: cereales, legumbres y patatas.
- Una dieta que contenga más de 300-400 g de fruta empezará a desplazar el equilibrio almidón/azúcares en favor de éstos.
- Los lácteos tienen una participación modesta en el aporte de glúcidos totales.
- La ingesta de azúcares contenidos en la fruta no puede compararse, desde muchos puntos de vista, con la de sacarosa («azúcar») como tal: el azúcar es una «caloría vacía», es decir, un producto desprovisto de cualquier otro factor nutricional más allá de la sacarosa; algo radicalmente distinto sucede con la fruta.
- La ingesta de «azúcar» tenderá a desequilibrar la relación almidón/azúcares.

¿Qué cantidad y tipo de glúcidos es recomendable tomar por la mañana?

El desayuno debe contener alrededor del 25 % del total de glúcidos diarios (330 / 4 = 82,5 g según el ejemplo anterior); de ellos, el mayor porcentaje será de almidón.

Todo ello se conseguirá, como veremos posteriormente, con las ingestas recomendadas de cereales, frutas y lácteos.

## *Grasas*

Las grasas son, de entre todos los componentes de la dieta, los más energéticos: 9 Cal / g. Su ingesta resulta fundamental, porque con ellas ingerimos ácidos grasos esenciales (que el organismo es incapaz de sintetizar) y por ser el vehículo de las vitaminas liposolubles (A, D, E y K), al tiempo que son necesarias para su correcta absorción intestinal. Además, las grasas confieren sabor y palatabilidad a nuestra alimentación.

En la actualidad se recomienda que las grasas aporten entre el 30 y el 35 % del VCT, centrándose las principales limitaciones en las grasas saturadas y poliinsaturadas (cada una no debe aportar más del 10 % del VCT), dejando un margen más amplio para las monoinsaturadas, cuyo máximo representante es el ácido oleico, el tipo de ácido graso que predomina en el aceite de oliva, razón por la que este producto se califica como cardiosaludable, siendo el producto estrella de la llamada dieta mediterránea.

La ingestión de grasas por la mañana presenta, pues, algunos aspectos poco favorables:

- Digestión más o menos laboriosa.
- Retraso de la llegada de glúcidos a la sangre.
- Reducción de espacio para los glúcidos ingeridos.

Todo ello dependerá, lógicamente, de la cantidad de grasas consumida.

### Proteínas

Las proteínas son las estructuras que ejecutan las funciones en las células; así, están implicadas en la regulación metabólica, el movimiento, las defensas, las estructuras de sostén..., que dependen de un buen balance proteico. La finalidad básica de las proteínas de la dieta es, en el caso del individuo adulto, reparar las obligadas pérdidas diarias de sus constituyentes básicos, los aminoácidos.

En el caso de los niños, las necesidades proteicas son, en relación con su peso corporal, mayores que en los adultos, debido a la formación de nuevos tejidos. En definitiva, un buen balance proteico exige la reposición diaria de aquello que se perdió y, en la fase de crecimiento, el aporte de materiales para hacerlo posible, lo que se conoce como balance nitrogenado positivo.

Las recomendaciones diarias actuales para un adulto se sitúan en 0,8 g / kg · día, aunque en la práctica se suelen elevar hasta 1 g. Por consiguiente, un individuo de 70 kg deberá ingerir 70 g de proteínas al día. Aquí también existe una recomendación cualitativa, basada en la diferente calidad de las proteínas procedentes de alimentos de origen animal y de origen vegetal; las primeras son más completas (proporciones de aminoácidos esenciales más ajustadas a nuestras necesidades) y presentan mejor digestibilidad. Se acepta, generalmente, que cada una proporciona el 50 % del total, lo que para el ejemplo anterior representaría 35 g de proteínas de origen animal y 35 g de proteínas de origen vegetal.

Puesto que el recambio de proteínas corporales, es decir, la relación entre la destrucción y la nueva síntesis, es constante, y no tenemos reservas proteicas, parece lógico que el organismo se beneficie de aportes regulares a lo largo del día, que serían perfectamente compatibles con los ritmos alimentarios que habitualmente se aconsejan.

El desayuno que se propone en la actualidad proporciona tanto proteínas de origen animal (productos lácteos) como de origen vegetal (cereales).

### Micronutrientes

En ellos están incluidos los minerales y las vitaminas, que desempeñan un papel fundamentalmente regulador. No proporcionan energía directamente al organismo, pero muchos de ellos están implicados en su obtención a partir de los glúcidos y grasas.

El metabolismo de los micronutrientes parece no estar sujeto a la necesidad de tener que integrar sus componentes específicamente en el desayuno. En consecuencia, no hay recomendaciones específicas sobre el consumo de estos nutrientes por la mañana. Ahora bien, un desayuno ausente o insuficiente puede provocar un aporte de micronutrientes inferior a las necesidades. Esta situación, que por frecuente ha sido bautizada por algunos expertos como «deficiencias en situación de abundancia», es una de las paradojas ligadas a la alimentación moderna.

Los estados nutricionales deficitarios en micronutrientes, más frecuentes de lo que podría pensarse, expresan hasta cierto punto el fracaso del modelo alimentario actual y subrayan que la abundancia y el exceso alimentario no basta para garantizar la ausencia de desequilibrios por defecto.

Con todo, una de las recomendaciones fundamentales para garantizar un aporte de micronutrientes adecuado es ingerir una dieta suficiente desde el punto de vista energético y proteico, y que sea, además, variada.

## ALIMENTOS BÁSICOS PARA PONERSE EN MARCHA

Actualmente se considera que un desayuno equilibrado se basa en una trilogía de alimentos básicos: frutas, cereales y lácteos.

### *Frutas*

Una de las características nutricionales más destacadas de las frutas es su elevado contenido en agua, que es siempre superior al 75 % y muy a menudo se sitúa entre el 85 y el 90 %. Pero el principal motivo por el que se recomienda tomar fruta en el desayuno es por su rico contenido en glúcidos, tratándose en este caso de azúcares. Éste es variable según las frutas (tabla 2).

No obstante, las frutas no son, como algunas veces se piensa, alimentos completos. Muchos nutrientes están muy mal representados y las necesidades de los mismos no podrían ser cubiertas adecuadamente si utilizáramos la fruta como alimento exclusivo. Así, por ejemplo, el contenido en proteínas rara vez alcanza el 1 %, al tiempo que el de grasas es aún inferior. Sin embargo, de todos es sabida la importancia que tienen, aunque unas más que otras, por su alto contenido en vitamina C; el consumo de fruta, junto con el de hortalizas frescas, resulta fundamental para cubrir las necesidades de esta vitamina hidrosoluble.

Las recomendaciones actuales de consumo de alimentos se efectúan en forma de raciones. ¿Qué se considera entonces una ración de fruta?: 150 g, lo que para frutas de tamaño medio muchas veces equivale a una pieza entera (manzana, naranja, melocotón, etc.). También un vaso de 200 cc de zumo de fruta natural se considera una ración.

La recomendación actual sobre el consumo de frutas es de un mínimo de dos raciones diarias, de las que preferentemente una será un cítrico. El desayuno se presenta como un momento ideal para su consumo.

Dado que cada día parece más evidente el papel protector que cumple este tipo de alimentos en patologías de alta prevalencia en nuestra población, estimular su consumo es una de las prioridades del consejo nutricional actual.

Algunos consejos sobre el consumo de frutas en el desayuno son:

- La fruta debe proceder, siempre que sea posible, de cultivos biológicos. Sólo entonces puede admitirse, cuando esté indicado, comerla con piel.
- Cualquier manipulación (pelado, rallado, licuado) a que se someta la fruta deberá realizarse inmediatamente antes de su consumo, a fin de preservar al máximo su contenido en micronutrientes. A este respecto conviene tener en cuenta que la vitamina C es la más sensible a los agentes físico-químicos.
- La fruta debe comerse cuando se halle en su punto ideal de sazón.
- Por supuesto, las frutas de la estación son las que mejor relación calidad/precio presentan.
- En invierno, tanto las piezas de fruta como sus zumos pueden templarse al baño María.

## TABLA 2. FRUTAS DE CONSUMO HABITUAL CON MAYOR CONTENIDO EN AZÚCARES (VALORES MEDIOS)

| Frutas | g /100 g |
|---|---|
| Plátano | 20 |
| Chirimoya | 20 |
| Uva | 16 |
| Higo | 16 |
| Cereza | 14 |
| Manzana | 12 |
| Piña | 11 |
| Ciruela | 11 |
| Níspero | 10,5 |
| Pera | 10,5 |
| Albaricoque | 9,5 |
| Melocotón | 9 |
| Naranja | 9 |
| Mandarina | 9 |

Nota: puesto que el principal macronutriente de la fruta son los glúcidos, su contenido energético depende en gran medida de la presencia de los mismos.

- No existe ningún argumento de peso para establecer un orden en la ingesta de fruta durante el desayuno: puede ser antes, durante o después, dependiendo de tolerancias y gustos personales.

- Si bien a veces se habla acerca de mezclas poco aconsejables, por ejemplo entre almidón (cereales) y ácidos (frutas), o entre leche y frutas, las tolerancias personales tienen la última palabra. Por lo general, estas mezclas suelen ser toleradas sin ningún problema por personas con sistemas digestivos funcionales.

### Cereales

Los cereales son el producto alimenticio más consumido en el mundo y constituyen la base de la alimentación humana. En concreto, dos de ellos se reparten el protagonismo a este respecto: el trigo y el arroz. Son alimentos con un alto contenido en glúcidos (almidón), y ello les otorga un papel destacado en el desayuno.

El interés nutricional de los cereales no termina aquí. Sus proteínas, que representan entre un 7 y un 10 %, si bien son deficientes en lisina, contribuyen a complementar el aporte proteico total. Además, caso de no añadírseles, los cereales tienen un contenido extremadamente bajo en grasas y nulo en colesterol, un lípido que es patrimonio exclusivo del reino animal.

Por lo demás, los cereales presentan también cantidades importantes de ciertos micronutrientes: tiamina (vitamina $B_1$), niacina (vitamina $B_3$), magnesio, hierro y en algunos casos zinc (pan integral en particular). Por contra, su contenido en vitaminas C, $B_{12}$ (únicamente presente en alimentos de origen animal), A y D es nulo.

En nuestra cultura, el principal cereal es el trigo, y no consumido como tal, sino tras la obtención

## TABLA 3. CONTENIDO EN ALMIDÓN DE CEREALES Y PRODUCTOS DERIVADOS

| Producto | g / 100 g |
|---|---|
| Arroz blanco | 86 |
| Pastas alimenticias | 82 |
| Harina de trigo | 80 |
| Biscotes | 78 |
| Arroz integral | 77 |
| Harina de maíz | 76 |
| Pan blanco | 58 |
| Pan integral | 49 |

de su harina, con la que se confeccionan diferentes productos entre los que destaca, fundamentalmente, el pan.

El pan es un alimento excelente cuya presencia diaria en la dieta es uno de los elementos que garantiza el equilibrio nutricional. Su contenido energético, tan discutido por aquéllos que defienden equivocadamente que «engorda», se debe fundamentalmente al almidón que contiene. En la actualidad, las autoridades sanitarias, a la vista del descenso espectacular de su consumo en las últimas décadas, recomiendan a la población que aumente el consumo de pan en detrimento de otros productos con mayor contenido en grasas. Se considera adecuada una ingesta de entre 150 y 200 g de pan diarios, así como su presencia en todas las comidas del día.

En el desayuno, el pan es un alimento opcional, en especial cuando en su composición sólo entran los componentes de la receta original: harina, levadura, agua y sal (aunque a veces se abuse de ella). Y es que, en efecto, la adición de sal al pan es tal que acaba siendo uno de los factores que limita su consumo (véase el apartado «Hipertensión»).

El pan integral, es decir, aquél elaborado con un grado de extracción del 100 %, presenta una riqueza en fibra y micronutrientes superior al pan blanco de uso habitual, cuyo grado de extracción se sitúa alrededor del 70 %, puesto que parte del grano se elimina. Con todo, hay que decir que los componentes externos del grano, presentes en el pan integral, disminuyen la disponibilidad de algunos micronutrientes, con lo que la diferencia más importante entre un tipo de pan y otro acaba siendo la de su contenido en fibra, que es el triple en el pan integral: 9 g frente a 3 g por cada 100 g de alimento. Dado que la presencia de fibra en nuestro modelo alimentario actual está muy a menudo lejos de lo que se recomienda, parece evidente que la ingesta de pan integral es beneficiosa. No obstante, su uso debe adaptarse a las distintas circunstancias considerando, por ejemplo, que la fibra de los cereales es bastante dura, y puede ser irritante para intestinos delicados y para los niños.

El llamado pan de molde industrial contiene a menudo grasas en su composición. A su vez, el contenido en azúcares es de 4-5 g / 100 g.

Algunos consejos sobre el consumo de pan en el desayuno:

• Es interesante alternar el consumo de pan de trigo con el de otros de buena calidad, en cuya composición entren harinas de otros cereales.

- El pan tostado no es «de régimen» y tiene, a igualdad de peso, más calorías que el pan tierno.
- Si al tostar en exceso el pan algunas partes se han carbonizado, deben eliminarse por completo.
- El pan congelado no pierde ninguna de sus características nutricionales.
- La toma de un bocadillo (literalmente bocado pequeño) a media mañana es una buena forma de completar un desayuno que pueda resultar insuficiente.

### Productos de bollería

Otro tipo de productos cuyo consumo preocupa, en este caso no por defecto sino por exceso, tiene también como base la harina de trigo pero con acompañantes no deseados, entre los que destacan las grasas. El principal reproche que se les hace a los productos de bollería es su elevado contenido en grasas, y en particular en grasas saturadas. Aceptando como denominador común un contenido demasiado elevado de estas grasas en los productos de bollería, existe bastante disparidad no tan sólo en función del tipo de producto, sino también en función del modo de elaboración; así, por ejemplo, las ensaimadas, los cruasanes, las magdalenas etc., pueden tener contenidos muy distintos en función de la forma en que se han elaborado. Se hace necesario, siempre que el producto se comercialice envasado, la lectura de la etiqueta. Con todo, es bastante habitual que 100 g de este tipo de productos proporcionen 10 g o más de grasas saturadas.

Pero, en la actualidad, no sólo preocupa la presencia de grasas saturadas, sino también la de los llamados ácidos grasos trans, un tipo de grasas insaturadas que no se encuentran en la naturaleza y que resultan de manipulaciones como la hidrogenación a la que se someten las materias primas grasas.

Datos publicados recientemente señalan que el consumo medio en Europa de ácidos grasos trans es inferior a 6 g / día, aunque ciertas personas consumen más de 12 g / día, cantidad que se considera que puede disminuir el col-HDL (conocido como colesterol «bueno») y aumentar el col-LDL (conocido como colesterol «malo») y el riesgo de arterioesclerosis. Hoy se cree necesario reducir el consumo de ácidos grasos trans especialmente en los niños y durante el embarazo. Algunos autores han reclamado la necesidad de que se indique en el etiquetado la cantidad de ácidos grasos trans presentes en el producto final.

La presencia frecuente de aditivos alimentarios en los productos de bollería, entre los que figuran los colorantes, no es, precisamente, un argumento favorable para estimular su consumo.

Un producto del que también ha aumentado su consumo, pero de línea diferente, son los llamados cereales para el desayuno. Un antecedente clásico y bien conocido son los copos, producto resultante de someter el grano mondado a la acción del vapor de agua, y posteriormente al laminado y tostado.

A pesar de que habitualmente consideramos los cereales para el desayuno como un tipo de alimentos con características muy similares, lo cierto es que presentan también diferencias muy notables en función del producto. Las consideraciones nutricionales más importantes que se deben tener en cuenta son:

- La base de estos productos son los cereales: harina de trigo, arroz, etc. En consecuencia, el nutriente cuantitativamente más importante es el almidón.

- Contienen azúcar en diferentes porcentajes según el producto. Normalmente se especifica en la etiqueta. Son más interesantes cuanto menos azúcar contengan.
- La presencia de grasas es variable. Debe prestarse atención al contenido en grasas saturadas y también a la presencia entre sus ingredientes de grasas hidrogenadas (ácidos grasos trans).
- El contenido en fibra puede variar mucho en función de la utilización de cereales integrales, refinados o mezclados.
- Si están elaborados únicamente con productos vegetales no contienen colesterol.
- Son productos con un bajo grado de humedad (poca agua). Por consiguiente, tienen un elevado contenido energético.
- El contenido en sodio es muy variable, pero en algunos es bastante elevado.
- Para aquéllos que están chocolateados, sería de interés que figurara en la etiqueta cuál es la cantidad de cacao utilizada. Probablemente, esto limitaría su consumo.
- Por su particular textura, son altamente pegajosos. Ello unido a la presencia de azúcar impone una adecuada higiene dental tras su consumo.
- Un argumento comercial es su enriquecimiento con algunos micronutrientes. Algo que no resulta necesario siempre que la dieta esté bien planificada.
- A pesar de que estos productos se destinan preferentemente al público infantil y adolescente, pueden ser consumidos a cualquier edad.
- En general poseen pocos aditivos. En todo caso debe preferirse aquel producto que no los contenga o que los contenga en menor cantidad.
- Son productos poco perecederos.

## ¿Patatas en el desayuno?

Desde la óptica nutricional las patatas podrían, perfectamente, formar parte de nuestro desayuno, salvo que, naturalmente, su modo de preparación lo desaconsejara, como sucede con las patatas fritas. Su riqueza en almidón, su ausencia de grasas y su fácil digestión así lo indican.

Sin embargo, su consumo no es habitual en ese momento del día, y ello es por algo más que por razones prácticas de tiempo (tampoco en días de fiesta o vacaciones las tomamos). Con ello queremos señalar que nuestros hábitos alimentarios se construyen con cierta independencia, y a veces, incluso a costa de las realidades nutricionales. Una evidencia más sobre la extraordinaria influencia que tiene la cultura sobre lo que comemos.

### Alimentos lácteos

Los alimentos lácteos constituyen un grupo de alimentos básicos constituido por la leche, las leches fermentadas y los quesos. Las dos características nutricionales principales de estos alimentos son su contenido en proteínas y calcio. Las proteínas de los alimentos lácteos son de excelente calidad, puesto que contienen todos los aminoácidos esenciales y tienen una elevada digestibilidad.

Por otro lado, es bien conocido el papel fundamental que desempeña el equilibrio cálcico en la dieta para preservar nuestra salud ósea. Las necesidades de calcio son elevadas, al tiempo que sus fuentes alimentarias importantes son escasas. Entre ellas destacan, qué duda cabe, los alimentos lácteos.

**TABLA 4. CONTENIDO MEDIO EN CALCIO DE ALGUNOS ALIMENTOS LÁCTEOS ÓPTIMOS PARA EL DESAYUNO**

| Alimento | mg Ca / 100 g |
|---|---|
| Queso Emmental y Gruyer[1] | 850 |
| Queso manchego (semicurado) | 800 |
| Queso fresco (de Burgos) | 191 |
| Yogur natural | 142 |
| Natillas | 140 |
| Leche desnatada[2] | 130 |
| Leche entera | 120 |
| Requesón | 60 |

Notas:
1: Los quesos contienen cantidades extraordinarias de calcio. En muchos casos, bastan 50 g para cubrir la mitad de las recomendaciones diarias de calcio de un adulto.
2: Si bien el valor de la leche parece pequeño, hay que tener en cuenta que la aportación real puede ser muy importante, considerando la cantidad de este alimento que se puede tomar. Ésta es una norma que se hace extensible a cualquier otro tipo de alimento.

En España, según una encuesta realizada por el Ministerio de Agricultura en 1988, de los 813 mg de calcio diarios ingeridos como media por los españoles, el 61,3 % procedía de productos lácteos. Pero es que, además, el calcio lácteo es muy bien absorbido a nivel intestinal. Este porcentaje disminuía hasta el 6,3 % cuando se trataba de frutas.

Otro nutriente menos conocido, en cuya cobertura los lácteos desempeñan un protagonismo especial, es la riboflavina o vitamina $B_2$. Una dieta que contenga dos raciones de lácteos a base de leche o yogur proporcionará el 64 % de las recomendaciones de esta vitamina para una mujer adulta. Esto resulta tanto más importante en la medida en que la riboflavina suele aparecer en las listas de las vitaminas «problemáticas».

El principal factor nutricional que limita la ingesta de lácteos es la grasa, no tanto por su cantidad, en especial si hablamos de leche y leches fermentadas, sino por su calidad. La calidad de las grasas de un alimento viene definida por su porcentaje de los diferentes tipos de ácidos grasos: saturados, monoinsaturados y poliinsaturados.

Lo cierto es que las grasas de los lácteos tienen un pésimo perfil, y ello es debido a la gran cantidad de grasas saturadas que contienen. Independientemente del producto lácteo al que nos refiramos, sus grasas contienen 20 veces más ácidos grasos saturados que poliinsaturados (cociente P / S = 0,05) y casi el doble de grasas saturadas que de insaturadas totales (cociente I / S = 0,58).

Dos raciones de lácteos al día aportarán entre 10 y 15 g de grasas saturadas, una cifra que se sitúa alrededor de la mitad de la cantidad máxima de estas grasas que se recomienda ingerir a diario.

El interés real de tomar lácteos desnatados descansa más en evitar el consumo de una cierta cantidad de grasas saturadas que sobre el aspecto, mucho más popular, de las calorías. Así, la leche desnatada está desprovista de grasas, y por ello su valor energético pasa a ser de 33 Cal / 100 ml, frente a las 65 Cal / 100 ml de la leche entera. Ello quiere decir que tomando 500 ml de leche diarios (dos raciones) tendremos un «ahorro» de 160 Cal. Pero, lo más importante, habremos tomado 10 g menos de grasas saturadas, de las que no se aconseja tomar mucho más de 20-25 g diarios.

Dado que en nuestra alimentación habitual, excesivamente cárnica y con presencia abundante de productos elaborados con abundancia de grasas saturadas, las grasas en general y las saturadas en particular suelen consumirse en cantidades mayores a las recomendadas, puede ser de interés general la ingestión de lácteos desnatados, aunque creemos que, puestos a reducir grasas, sería mucho mejor reducir y/o prescindir de las otras fuentes de grasas saturadas, y tomar la leche u otros lácteos con todo su sabor.

De todas formas, el consumo de leche desnatada, y también el de algunos de sus derivados desnatados, permite mantener las garantías de un consumo de calcio adecuado sin una sobrecarga de grasas saturadas, lo cual cobra un especial interés en determinados casos.

Es cierto que la eliminación de la grasa láctea conlleva también la de las vitaminas liposolubles y casi la totalidad del colesterol que contiene el producto original. Lo segundo es una ventaja; ahora bien, las consecuencias prácticas de lo primero no son excesivamente negativas, considerando que:

• La vitamina A, con diferencia la principal vitamina liposoluble de la leche, puede obtenerse sin un consumo adicional de grasas ingiriendo hortalizas frescas ricas en beta-caroteno (zanahorias), que se transforma en esta vitamina en nuestro organismo.

- La cantidad de vitamina D en la leche, una vitamina que podemos sintetizar en nuestra piel gracias a la acción de la luz solar, es extremadamente pequeña.

Con todo, el mercado ofrece actualmente productos desnatados enriquecidos con ambas vitaminas, e incluso con otros nutrientes. Pueden ser de interés especial en determinadas circunstancias.

Por otro lado, un factor nutricional que puede limitar el consumo de leche es, precisamente, el único azúcar que contiene en cantidad importante: la lactosa, que en la leche se encuentra en concentraciones del 4,5 al 5 %.

Después de la primera infancia o durante la adolescencia, son muchos los individuos que pierden, en mayor o menor medida, la capacidad de romper la lactosa a nivel intestinal, un paso absolutamente necesario para la posterior absorción de sus componentes; ello conduce a una serie de molestias intestinales que pueden presentarse tras su ingestión: gases, dolores abdominales, diarrea... Es la llamada intolerancia a la lactosa. Esta reacción adversa a la ingesta de leche depende siempre de la relación entre la cantidad de alimento ingerido y la capacidad de digestión de la lactosa, lo cual establece siempre una ecuación personal que el individuo podrá conocer con facilidad debido a la rápida presentación de los síntomas. La intolerancia a la lactosa no es una alergia alimentaria, pues en ella no media ningún mecanismo inmunológico.

El yogur, que contiene una cantidad de lactosa próxima a la de la leche, suele resultar mucho menos problemático en estos casos. Algunos experimentos han mostrado que la respuesta puede deberse a la capacidad lactásica de los propios microorganismos vivos de este producto alimenticio. El yogur es un excelente alimento que nos ofrece prestaciones inasequibles para la leche como, por ejemplo, una mejor digestibilidad general y la presencia de microorganismos benéficos, que pueden contribuir al mantenimiento de una flora intestinal óptima para nuestros intereses.

El queso, en cambio, no contiene lactosa. Si bien existen importantes diferencias entre las múltiples variedades de queso, en general podemos decir que, en relación con la leche y leches fermentadas, en este tipo de producto disminuye el contenido en agua, aumenta el contenido en grasas (de las que se mantiene el perfil), y también en proteínas, mientras que la lactosa está ausente. Se trata, pues, de un producto más calórico y, en la inmensa mayoría de ocasiones, más salado. Al mismo tiempo, su nivel de colesterol es muy considerable. El contenido en calcio es superior, y en muchos quesos muy superior (véase tabla 4), si bien debe tenerse en cuenta que por sus propias características nutricionales es un alimento del que sólo se deben consumir pequeñas cantidades; su patrón de consumo queda expresado de forma genial en el refrán popular: «Cada día queso y al año un queso».

Para la población adulta española se recomiendan dos raciones de alimentos lácteos diarias. En la tabla 5 aparecen las distintos ejemplos de raciones.

Algunos consejos para el consumo de alimentos lácteos en el desayuno son:

• La leche UHT es un producto que ha sido sometido a un tratamiento térmico enérgico de muy corta duración que permite una larga conserva-

| TABLA 5. EJEMPLOS DE RACIONES EQUIVALENTES DE ALIMENTOS LÁCTEOS |
| --- |
| Una taza de leche (250 cc). |
| Dos unidades de yogur (250 g) u otra leche fermentada. |
| 120 g de queso fresco. |
| 40-50 g de queso curado. |
| Nota: las recomendaciones pueden obtenerse con cualquiera de las múltiples combinaciones de las distintas raciones propuestas. |

ción. Ahora bien, una vez abierto el envase, debe conservarse en frío y consumirse en no mucho más de 24 horas.

- Para una leche conservada en perfectas condiciones higiénicas resulta inútil la ebullición, al tiempo que con ella se modifican negativamente sus características organolépticas.
- El yogur es un producto ligeramente ácido debido a la presencia de ácido láctico, producto de la fermentación, pero ello no significa que sea un producto acidificante. El límite de su ingesta es el mismo que el de los alimentos lácteos; dicho de otra manera: todas las raciones de lácteos del día pueden consumirse en forma de yogur.
- El yogur, como otras leches fermentadas o la misma leche, puede calentarse al baño María para templar su temperatura fría, necesaria para su adecuada conservación (a excepción de la leche UHT antes de que se abra el envase). No obstante, se debe proceder con cuidado, pues un calentamiento mucho más allá de los 40 °C puede des-

truir los microorganismos vivos que contiene, que son en gran parte responsables de sus efectos benéficos.

- Algunas preparaciones de queso fresco contienen mucha sal, lo que puede generar algunas contraindicaciones: úlceras gastroduodenales, hipertensión... Esta cuestión también deberá valorarse en el caso de la alimentación infantil.
- Fresco o curado, el queso puede entrar a formar parte del desayuno de personas sanas.

Entre los derivados lácteos que hemos citado no se encuentran ni la nata ni la mantequilla. Lo cierto es que estos productos, procedentes también de la leche, no presentan las mismas características nutricionales básicas y no pueden incluirse por ello en este grupo.

La mantequilla es un alimento muy graso (83 %), que sigue manteniendo el mismo perfil de grasas del producto del que proviene; además, su contenido en colesterol es muy notable: 230 mg / 100 g. Ello no quiere decir que la mantequilla (10 g, por ejemplo) no pueda ser utilizada más o menos ocasionalmente en el desayuno de personas sanas. Pero es un producto que no aporta ningún nutriente de interés en contraposición a sus grasas.

Para la nata sirven los mismos comentarios, pero considerando que contiene unos 30 g menos de grasa por cada 100 g de producto.

La margarina vegetal, que es un sustituto económico de la mantequilla pero no un derivado lácteo, no presenta el mismo interés que los productos a partir de los que se elabora. Así, por ejemplo, la margarina que se obtiene del aceite de girasol presenta una mayor saturación que la de dicho aceite, pues la solidificación del producto requiere una hidrogenación (saturación) más o menos importante de sus grasas.

Tampoco es un derivado lácteo la llamada «leche de soja», un alimento de composición distinta y que no se puede considerar un producto equivalente a la leche de vaca.

Otro producto de origen animal que se incluye a veces en el desayuno es el huevo. Salvo frito, es un alimento de fácil y rápida digestión, y una fuente de proteínas de excelente calidad, aunque de él no se puede esperar aporte ninguno de glúcidos. El factor limitante de su consumo es el contenido en colesterol de su yema, lo cual fija sus recomendaciones de ingesta en tres o cuatro huevos por semana en las personas sanas. Teniendo en cuenta estas consideraciones, puede introducirse en el desayuno (preferiblemente uno por toma) al que puede aportar variedad y valor nutritivo. Por último, para valorar la ingesta total de huevos deben considerarse las preparaciones que puedan incluirlos (flanes, pastelería, bollería, etc).

### Otros alimentos

Frutas, cereales y lácteos son los alimentos básicos del desayuno. No obstante, existen otros muchos alimentos que pueden estar presentes, precisamente con la función de complemento, en el desayuno. Su empleo puede proporcionar sabor, color y variedad, pero deben incluirse con la prudencia que su elevado contenido en grasas y/o azúcares aconseje. Es el caso de mermeladas, chocolates, azúcar...

Desde un punto de vista nutricional, su principal ventaja es el aporte de sabor y la incitación a comer otros alimentos importantes para el equilibrio

## Las prisas

Si algo no falta por la mañana son prisas. Las prisas son proporcionales al margen de tiempo que dejamos entre el momento en que nos levantamos y el momento en que empiezan nuestros horarios inaplazables. Habitualmente, en nuestras manos sólo está modificar la primera de las variables, pero nadie niega las dificultades de esa tarea. Sin embargo, bien mirado, los efectos negativos del estrés, los nervios y la mala nutrición sobrepasan con creces los beneficios de estar 20 o 30 minutos más en la cama y éste es, precisamente, el tiempo que necesitamos para un desayuno normal.

El desayuno es una de las grandes víctimas del sueño. Dejar preparada la mesa la noche anterior, llevar a cabo todas aquellas manipulaciones de los alimentos que no comprometan su valor nutricional (dejar la fruta lavada y seca, dejar en la mesa alimentos que no necesiten del frío para su conservación, convenientemente protegidos) y reservar un rincón especial del armario a fin de localizar todos los utensilios necesarios rápidamente..., son algunas estrategias para arrancarle algunos minutos al reloj.

nutricional, en especial en comensales «difíciles». Prescindiendo de dogmas y obsesiones, cabe decir que su consumo prudente no desequilibrará una dieta que esté bien planificada. Asociados al placer, estos alimentos son a menudo sometidos a juicios morales que se racionalizan con argumentos nutricionales. Es un error que se comete a menudo. Como señala Vincent: «La fisiología demuestra que la búsqueda del placer conduce a la moderación».

En definitiva, un desayuno como el que se recomienda actualmente nos sitúa en las mejores condiciones, no sólo para empezar bien el día, sino también, y en lo que a nutrición se refiere, para respetar el equilibrio de los macronutrientes (glúcidos, grasas y proteínas) y de los micronutrientes. Y es que un buen desayuno proporcionará cantidades significativas de vitaminas A, C y también de muchos de los componentes del grupo B ($B_1$, $B_2$, $B_3$, $B_{12}$...), así como de minerales como calcio, magnesio, hierro y zinc, cuyo equilibrio está más amenazado.

# TABLA 6. ANÁLISIS NUTRICIONAL DE UN DESAYUNO TIPO

| Alimentos | Cal. | Glúc. (g) | Gras. (g) | Prot. (g) | Fib. (g) | Col. (mg) | Ca (mg) | Fe (mg) | Vit. A (mg) | Vit. $B_2$ (mg) | Vit C (mg) |
|---|---|---|---|---|---|---|---|---|---|---|---|
| Zumo de naranja (200 ml) | 84 | 20 | 0,2 | 1,2 | 0,2 | 0 | 38 | 0,4 | 60 | 0 | 80 |
| Pan integral (100 g) | 228 | 49 | 1,4 | 8 | 8,5 | 0 | 21 | 2,5 | 0 | 0,1 | 0 |
| Requesón (120 g) | 115 | 1,7 | 4,8 | 16 | 0 | 30 | 72 | 0,1 | 45,5 | 0,24 | 0 |
| Miel (10 g) | 30 | 8 | 0 | 0,1 | 0 | 0 | 0,5 | 0,1 | 0 | 0 | 0 |
| Total | 457 | 78,7 | 6,4 | 25,3 | 8,7 | 30 | 131,5 | 3,1 | 105,5 | 0,34 | 80 |

- Considerando una dieta de 2.000 Cal, este desayuno aportaría el 23 % del VCT.
- Los glúcidos aportan el 68 % del total de Calorías del mismo.
- Del total de glúcidos, 29,7 g corresponden a azúcares.
- El total de grasas saturadas es de 3 g.
- Asumiendo que las necesidades proteicas diarias sean de 60 g, el desayuno cubre algo más del 40 %.
- Las proteínas de origen animal representan el 64 % del total ingerido.

- El contenido en fibra está próximo a la tercera parte de las recomendaciones diarias.
- Aporta sólo el 10 % de la ingesta máxima de colesterol recomendada.
- Si el aporte de calcio procediera de una ración de leche (250 ml) en lugar de requesón, (la fuente más pobre indicada en la tabla 3), el aporte de calcio alcanzaría los 300 mg.
- El zumo de naranja proporciona por sí solo 20 mg más del total de vitamina C recomendada diariamente para un adulto.

# EL DESAYUNO A LO LARGO DEL CICLO VITAL

Una vez expuestas las recomendaciones actuales sobre el desayuno y las bases fisiológicas sobre las que descansa, será conveniente abordar algunas particularidades que se dan en las distintas situaciones de la vida que, si bien no modifican las grandes líneas de lo propuesto, merecen una especial atención. La glucosa centra gran parte del protagonismo en estos casos, pues tanto sus aportes como sus necesidades se modifican a lo largo del ciclo vital.

## LA INFANCIA

Todos los intereses de un buen desayuno confluyen en la infancia, dadas las características de este período. Ésta es la razón por la que el desayuno de nuestros pequeños ha sido objeto de atención por parte de los organismos de Salud Pública mediante programas de educación nutricional.

Y es que en esta época de la vida es cuando se establecen gran parte de los hábitos alimentarios que perdurarán a lo largo de la misma y que determinarán, en gran medida, la futura salud o enfermedad del individuo adulto. En este sentido, el profesor Debry, de la Universidad de Nancy (Francia), señalaba en un informe sobre educación nutricional de la UE: «Es durante la infancia cuando la manera de alimentarse tiene más repercusiones, tanto favorables como desfavorables, respecto al futuro».

Ello sucede en una etapa en la que el equilibrio nutricional es precario, si consideramos las exigencias y las necesidades de los pequeños. Se deben, pues, cuidar en extremo todos los detalles: selección de alimentos, preparaciones adecuadas, ritmos alimentarios... Naturalmente, para todos ellos el desayuno es importante; no obstante, queremos incidir aquí sobre la importancia de la fragmentación de las tomas. La necesidad que tiene el niño de fragmentar su ingesta se basa en tres supuestos básicos:

- Necesidades nutricionales elevadas.
- Capacidad digestiva *in crescendo*.
- Capacidad limitada de soportar periodos de ayuno.

Los niños tienen, en función del crecimiento que experimentan, unas necesidades nutricionales que, expresadas en relación con el peso corporal, son mayores que en la etapa adulta; la ingesta media de calorías en la primera infancia cuadriplica, cuando se compara con el peso corporal, la de los adultos. Piénsese en este dato: los aproximadamente 650 ml de leche diarios que una madre ofrece a su bebé de mes y medio de edad equivaldrían a 10 litros para un adulto de 65 kg.

Todo ello, con un tubo digestivo que aún necesita madurar y cuya capacidad funcional es evidentemente menor que la de un adulto. Esta realidad fisiológica es bien conocida y condiciona no sólo el tipo de alimentos que puede tomar, sino también sus presentaciones y el ritmo de sus ingestas.

Finalmente, en relación con el último aspecto, un niño no tiene la misma capacidad metabólica que un adulto para hacer frente al ayuno. Teniendo en cuenta sus proporciones corporales, en particular el tamaño relativo de su cerebro en relación con el del adulto y las necesidades de glucosa de este órgano, se podrá deducir fácilmente que el equilibrio glucémico del niño es mucho más frágil; en este sentido conviene recordar que mientras el porcentaje del peso del cerebro respecto al del cuerpo es del 11 % a la edad de un año, desciende al 2 % en el adulto.

Por todo ello, existe una clara evidencia de que saltarse el desayuno es particularmente nefasto para el niño. El desayuno es una de las cuatro ingestas básicas que debe realizar el niño durante el día.

Es necesario volver a incidir aquí en el riesgo potencial ligado a una ingesta excesiva de grasas saturadas, debido a un consumo elevado de bollería que las incluya entre sus ingredientes. En este sentido, la Fundación Española del Corazón ha señalado que los malos hábitos alimentarios, que se adquieren durante la infancia, fomentan las patologías cardíacas; en concreto, los cardiólogos españoles piden que los niños consuman menos grasas saturadas.

A este respecto, una de las preguntas que se plantean a menudo los padres es: ¿deben tomar los alimentos lácteos, fundamentalmente leche y yogur, desnatados? La respuesta no es, como muy a menudo sucede en nutrición, positiva o negativa de forma taxativa, sino que depende de otros factores. Y es que, en efecto, para un niño cuya alimentación esté bien planificada y no consuma alimentos suplementarios con un exceso de grasas saturadas, el consumo de desnatados puede representar un triple error:

- Eliminación innecesaria de un constituyente energético de la dieta.
- Pérdida de una fuente alimentaria con vitamina A (si es que el producto alternativo no está enriquecido), lo cual puede ser particularmente importante en el mundo infantil poco amante del consumo de hortalizas (fuente de beta-carotenos).
- Menor satisfacción por pérdida de sabor.

Otra cosa muy distinta sería si la dieta estuviera sobrecargada de grasas saturadas y/o el niño presentara un nivel de colesterol elevado, condiciones ambas en las que estaría indicado el consumo de desnatados.

Con todo, sin grasa o con grasa, la ingesta de alimentos lácteos resulta esencial para el equilibrio nutricional del niño; en esta etapa se recomiendan más raciones diarias de alimentos lácteos que en la etapa adulta; en consecuencia, su presencia en el desayuno será más crítica. El volumen de las raciones se adaptará a la edad y a cada caso concreto, pero puede ser de 200 ml de leche o su equivalente a partir de 1-2 años.

Por diferentes motivos, que tienen como denominador común su aporte de glúcidos y su prácticamente nulo contenido en grasas, resulta también fundamental la presencia de cereales y frutas, con lo cual la conclusión es obvia: es necesario contar con todos los alimentos básicos para un buen desayuno. La ración de frutas puede ser equivalente a la del adulto, mientras que la de cereales generalmente será inferior debido a las menores necesidades energéticas absolutas del pequeño; a esta edad el hambre suele ser una guía segura, lo que quedará corroborado si se acompaña de un crecimiento y un peso adecuados.

Una ventaja adicional de estos alimentos es la de poder ser consumidos sin aditivos alimentarios. En este sentido, resulta particularmente polémico el uso de colorantes, muy a menudo empleados en alimentación infantil por su efecto comercial. En general podemos decir que la alimentación infantil, con más motivo aún que la de los adultos, debe estar lo más libre posible de aditivos alimentarios.

Así pues, adaptado a las diversas circunstancias, el patrón de desayuno propuesto será una buena base para construir al equilibrio nutricional del día.

En caso de que, por cualquier motivo, se fragmente la ingesta con una toma a media mañana, lo que puede ser una buena medida a ciertas edades, se debe tener especial cuidado en no ingerir una cantidad importante de alimento cuando no haya un espacio horario suficiente para hacer su digestión. Así ocurre generalmente cuando utilizamos el servicio de comedor de la escuela, que suele empezar, con buen criterio, por los más pequeños, ya que son los más necesitados de dicha fragmentación. Un niño que a la hora del patio haya comido algo más que una colación, es muy probable que no tenga hambre a la hora de comer, alterándose a partir de aquí todo su ritmo diario de comidas.

## LA ADOLESCENCIA

En la adolescencia se produce la segunda gran etapa de crecimiento rápido del organismo. Pero al margen de crecer, en el adolescente se producen otros muchos cambios morfológicos y funcionales que exigen aportes adecuados de nutrientes: aumento de los depósitos de grasa en el tejido subcutáneo, incremento de la masa muscular, aumento del volumen de sangre y maduración sexual. Todo ello hace que un adolescente necesite, en cifras absolutas, más nutrientes que un adulto de su propio sexo. Se trata, pues, de un período nutricional crítico.

Pero no terminan aquí los cambios; en la esfera psicológica se producirán enormes sacudidas que, en algunos casos, pueden poner en peligro la cobertura nutricional. Así, el adolescente intentará romper con hábitos y costumbres alimentarias aprendidos durante años con los padres, se hará miembro de pandillas y adoptará como uno de los códigos de identificación con las mismas un comportamiento alimentario particular.

Los espectaculares cambios corporales propios de esta etapa, ligados a la tiránica presión que existe en nuestros días sobre el modelo corporal, conducen muy a menudo a los adolescentes, aunque mucho más a las chicas que a los chicos, a alteraciones alimentarias. Éstas tienen múltiples manifestaciones, de diferente gravedad y consecuencias muy variables, pero es muy frecuente la alteración de los ritmos alimentarios.

Pero los cambios no sólo afectarán a la posible adopción de un régimen, a la eliminación de alguna comida o a la alteración de los ritmos alimentarios, sino que a ello habrá que añadir el consumo de alimentos superfluos, de bebidas refrescantes, la iniciación de la ingesta de alcohol, la redefinición de gustos y aversiones...

No hay duda de que la mayor autonomía supone un mayor número de comidas fuera de casa, lo cual facilita la adquisición de alimentos inadecuados y dificulta la de los adecuados y, además, disminuye la posibilidad de control por parte de los padres.

Se trata de una etapa de grandes tensiones en la que, en gran medida, el éxito dependerá de esfuerzos anteriores. En particular, y en lo que respecta a la alimentación, recogeremos aquí los frutos del tipo de educación nutricional que hayamos proporcionado a nuestro/a hijo/a.

Por todas estas razones, el desayuno puede resultar una ingesta particularmente comprometida; por contra, como siempre que aumentan las necesidades nutricionales, tiene aquí un papel muy especial para la adquisición de un buen equilibrio nutricional.

En la adolescencia, el aporte de alimentos lácteos para obtener una ingesta de calcio suficiente es fundamental y constituye uno de los períodos en los que se recomienda que sea mayor: tres o cuatro raciones diarias. Ello es así porque la adolescencia es una época decisiva en la construcción del armazón óseo, sobre el cual se apoyará el organismo. Durante esta fase de adquisición neta de hueso, los aportes de calcio adecuados, acompañados naturalmente de los demás equilibrios nutricionales, favorecerán la máxima expresión del crecimiento óseo, inscrita en el programa genético propio de cada individuo.

También es cierto que un consumo adecuado de frutas y hortalizas aportará un contingente importante de las vitaminas necesarias. Sin embargo, el consumo de estos alimentos de buena calidad es difícil fuera de casa. Por contra, los cereales, en especial preparaciones derivadas de la harina de trigo, suelen estar presentes en cantidad importante en la dieta del adolescente, aunque lamentablemente demasiado a menudo unidos a grasas, azúcares y aditivos.

Es cierto que las dietas que necesitan un mayor número de calorías, como en el caso del adolescente, admiten mayor cantidad de alimentos complementarios, es decir, no básicos, pero suele ser frecuente que el consumo de aquéllos se produzca a expensas de éstos. Con todo, y salvo en situaciones alarmantes, no debemos ser demasiado rígidos con el modelo alimentario de los adolescentes. A veces, puede ser peor el enfrentamiento que los potenciales desórdenes que intentamos evitar.

## EL EMBARAZO

La nutrición es tan importante para la reproducción que ésta no puede llevarse a cabo sin un aporte adecuado de alimento. El embarazo es un período en el que aumentan de forma notable las necesidades nutricionales. Este incremento se debe, por una parte, a las demandas del feto y, por otra, a la formación de nuevas estructuras maternas necesarias para la gestación (placenta, útero, glándulas mamarias, sangre), así como para la formación de depósitos energéticos que contribuirán a garantizar las demandas de energía del posparto y la lactancia.

La adaptación a esa nueva situación conlleva modificaciones en el metabolismo materno; el caso de los glúcidos es particularmente importante, considerando que la glucosa desempeña un papel primordial en el crecimiento fetal. Una de las traducciones alimentarias importantes de estos cambios es la necesidad de evitar que transcurran demasiadas horas sin tomar alimentos, pues puede producirse hipoglucemia y una movilización importante de las grasas de reserva que provoca cetonemia (aumento de los cuerpos cetónicos en la sangre). Ambas situaciones revierten con la ingesta de alimentos con glúcidos.

En este marco resulta fundamental repartir bien las comidas a lo largo del día, y muy en especial tomar un desayuno completo, sobre todo al final del embarazo, que es la época más delicada en este sentido. Lo preferible es que se distribuyan los alimentos en cinco comidas diarias; así, el desayuno puede representar el 20 % del total energético, si bien el modelo, en cuanto a tipos de alimentos, no debe variar prácticamente en nada al de la misma mujer antes de su embarazo. Se recomienda una toma a media mañana que puede representar el 10 % del total energético, y puede estar constituida también a base de algún alimento lácteo, y fruta o bocadillo.

Durante el embarazo se aconseja un mayor consumo de alimentos lácteos: tres raciones diarias; desnatados o no, en función de la evolución del peso y la salud de la futura mamá. Todas las frutas frescas pueden tomarse a condición de que sean de la máxima calidad (preferiblemente biológicas). Los cereales continúan estando en la base del equilibrio nutricional. Es recomendable no abusar de la bollería confeccionada con excesivas grasas y azúcar.

## LA LACTANCIA

Las necesidades nutricionales durante la lactancia son, en su conjunto, superiores a las del embarazo, puesto que la madre va a continuar alimentando a su hijo, pero ahora el alimento se vehicula a través de las glándulas mamarias en lugar del cordón umbilical; la madre lactante va a segregar alrededor de 650-800 ml diarios de leche, un líquido lo suficientemente nutritivo como para permitir que su bebé duplique su peso en seis meses.

El ritmo de ingesta del pequeño durante las primeras semanas ocasionará también que la madre modifique sus ritmos de sueño y de alimentación, máxime si se respeta el patrón primitivo con que se amamantaba a los lactantes, es decir, según su demanda, lo cual aún se observa en algunas culturas primitivas y mucho más esporádicamente entre nosotros. No obstante, a medida que el niño empieza a adaptarse a los períodos vigilia-sueño normales, la dieta de la madre también se podrá planificar mejor.

Todavía con más motivo que durante el embarazo, será recomendable repartir la ingesta total de comida en cinco o seis veces. Especialmente el desayuno, y en menor medida la toma de media mañana, resultan fundamentales para garantizar el equilibrio nutricional.

Al igual que durante el embarazo, se aconseja incrementar el consumo de alimentos lácteos, siendo de tres a cuatro las raciones diarias que se recomiendan, aumentando, pues, el interés de su presencia en el desayuno. Todas las frutas están permitidas. En cuanto al consumo de cereales, se desaconseja nuevamente aquellas preparaciones que contengan excesivas grasas y azúcar.

Durante la lactancia, la madre debe evitar el consumo de diversos productos que pueden pasar a la leche y alterar su sabor, y/o ser perjudiciales para el pequeño. De entre ellos, uno de los más habituales en el desayuno es el café, con su alcaloide la cafeína.

## LA ACTIVIDAD DEPORTIVA

Los deportistas tienen unas necesidades nutricionales superiores a las de las personas sedentarias. La magnitud de este aumento estará en relación con el tiempo y la intensidad con la que se practica el deporte.

Así, por ejemplo, aumentan las necesidades energéticas, un aumento que debe compensarse ingiriendo fundamentalmente más glúcidos, y es que, si bien los glúcidos son importantes para todos, aún lo son más para los deportistas. Hoy está admitido que el rendimiento deportivo, y muy en particular el de las prácticas aeróbicas, depende de las reservas de glucógeno muscular que, a su vez, están en relación directa con la cantidad de glúcidos presentes en la dieta. Una dieta rica en glúcidos puede retrasar la aparición de la fatiga, y es la que siguen deportistas de alto nivel en especialidades tan duras como la maratón o el ciclismo en carretera.

Conviene recordar aquí que, a excepción de la leche y leches fermentadas, que como ya se ha indicado tienen un reducido contenido en lactosa, todos los glúcidos que consumimos proceden de alimentos de origen vegetal. Por consiguiente, el deportista hará bien en vegetalizar su dieta, dando prioridad a alimentos tales como cereales, legumbres, patatas y frutas, lo cual contribuirá también a minimizar dos de los errores más frecuentes que se observan en la alimentación de este colectivo: ingesta excesiva de proteínas y de grasas.

En este contexto, el desayuno se convierte en un momento esencial para recargar las reservas del glucógeno. En cuanto al aspecto cualitativo, el desayuno del deportista no tiene que ser muy diferente del recomendado en general, siendo la base la misma. Por contra, puede aumentar la cantidad de alimento, en especial si las necesidades energéticas son superiores a las 3.000 Cal diarias. En la tabla 7 se recoge un modelo de desayuno para un deportista con un gasto energético de 3.000 Cal.

71

## TABLA 7. MODELO DE INGESTA DE COMIDA MATINAL PARA UN DEPORTISTA QUE CONSUMA 3.000 CALORÍAS DIARIAS

**Desayuno**

- Un vaso de zumo de frutas (200 cc).
- Una taza de leche desnatada (250 cc).
- Una cucharada pequeña de miel o azúcar (10 g).
- Una taza de cereales (60 g).
- Una ración de pan (60 g).
- 30-40 g de queso fresco.

**A media mañana**

- Un yogur desnatado.
- Una ración de fruta (125 g).
- Una cucharada pequeña de miel (10 g).

Nota: la presencia de lácteos desnatados en la dieta del deportista tiene como finalidad dejar más «espacio» a los glúcidos.

## LA VEJEZ

Los ancianos son el principal grupo de riesgo de déficit nutricional en los países ricos. Ello resulta fácil de comprender si se observa que, por un lado, múltiples factores se interponen en sus ingestas y aportes adecuados: falta de recursos económicos, invalidez, depresión, soledad, pérdida de apetito y menor eficacia de los procesos nutricionales; por otro lado, con los datos actuales, se considera que las recomendaciones nutricionales para las personas mayores deben ser, energía aparte, muy similares si no iguales, a las de los adultos jóvenes, o lo que es lo mismo, se admite que las necesidades nutricionales no disminuyen, o lo hacen poco, en relación con la edad.

Un par de ejemplos relacionados con la ingesta de fruta bastarán para ilustrar las dificultades que se presentan en esta etapa de la vida.

Las capacidades digestivas menguan con la edad, comenzando por el estado dental y terminando por la motilidad del colon. Este problema puede necesitar de modificaciones alimentarias que permitan solucionarlo, alterando lo mínimo posible el estado nutricional del anciano. Así, una dentadura deficiente dificultará tomar las piezas de fruta. En consecuencia, la textura de los alimentos deberá modificarse a fin de no vernos obligados a suprimir cierto tipo de alimentos que, por otro lado, resultan fundamentales para un adecuado equilibrio nutricional.

Ciertos problemas motores pueden limitar la capacidad de realizar ciertas operaciones, como por ejemplo pelar la fruta o hacer zumos. En tal caso, si no existe la posibilidad de una ayuda externa, los zumos comerciales pueden ser una buena solución. Los lácteos son un alimento de fácil consumo que apenas necesitan preparación y resultan económicos. En el terreno nutricional, continúan siendo la fuente fundamental de calcio que han venido representando durante toda la vida. Para los ancianos, aparte del calcio, son una fuente inestimable de proteínas de calidad, vitamina A (si se toman enteros), vitaminas $B_2$ y $B_{12}$ (en especial los quesos) y de zinc, un nutriente que suele ser deficiente en esta etapa vital y que desempeña un papel crucial en la defensa del organismo ante agresiones externas. No obstante, su consumo no debe superar las dos o tres raciones diarias.

En cuanto a los cereales, puede ser necesario recurrir a alimentos con una textura blanda que no exijan demasiada fragmentación mecánica. La leche, cuando se consume, puede servir para ablandar algunos de los alimentos elegidos. La bollería sin excesivas grasas (brioches, magdalenas, etc.) son una solución, aunque siempre debe procurarse una adecuada selección de aquellos productos con un perfil graso más favorable.

Cuando se piensa en la dieta del anciano, debe tenerse muy en cuenta que, con la edad, se produce una pérdida parcial de las capacidades sensoriales; muy en particular la disminución del sentido del gusto, que actúa desfavorablemente en relación con una adecuada nutrición. Por ello los menús no sólo deben ser equilibrados, sino también atractivos y apetecibles. También debe valorarse de forma ligeramente distinta a como se hacía en la etapa adulta la relación beneficios/riesgos de la ingesta de algunos alimentos o condimentos, como la sal y el azúcar. Y es que, en ocasiones, habrá más riesgo de deficiencia nutricional si el anciano deja de comer o come menos cantidad de algún alimento, a causa de su escasa sapidez, que debido a la ingesta de algún componente alimentario que le proporcione sabor al alimento. Resulta difícil hacer aquí generalizaciones y lo óptimo será individualizar cada caso.

La propia disminución de las funciones digestivas impedirá consumir volúmenes importantes de comida de una sola vez. Ésta es una de las principales razones por las que el desayuno se convierte en pieza clave del equilibrio nutricional del anciano. El desayuno, siguiendo las directrices generales mencionadas y adaptándolas a cada realidad, será la primera de las cuatro o cinco tomas diarias de alimento que garantizarán una adecuada nutrición en la última etapa de la vida.

# LOS DIVERSOS TRASTORNOS Y EL DESAYUNO

Las pautas hasta aquí señaladas han hecho siempre referencia, excepto cuando se ha hecho alguna mención específica, a situaciones fisiológicas normales, es decir, a individuos sanos.

A continuación queremos hacer mención de aquellas modificaciones más importantes que se aconsejan en algunos de los trastornos más frecuentes que se presentan en nuestra sociedad, y que son considerados como problemas de salud pública. Es necesario, sin embargo, advertir que, en la totalidad de los casos, se trata de trastornos multifactoriales, es decir, que sus causas desencadenantes pueden ser múltiples.

## OBESIDAD

La obesidad es una situación en la que se produce un exceso de peso como consecuencia de un cúmulo excesivo de grasa en el cuerpo. Puesto que la grasa es la gran reserva energética del organismo, podemos deducir que en esta situación lo que se produce en última instancia es un balance energético positivo, es decir, unas entradas superiores a las salidas. Si bien éste es el principio termodinámico infalible de esta situación, no es menos cierto que sus causas pueden ser múltiples y no son aún del todo conocidas.

¿Cuándo se está obeso? Desde un punto de vista sanitario, se admite que la definición más simple del peso ideal viene determinada por el llamado Índice de Masa Corporal (IMC):

$$IMC = \frac{P}{T^2}$$

donde P es el peso (en kg) y T la talla (en m). Para el adulto se considera un peso normal cualquiera que dé, como resultado de la aplicación de esta fórmula, un valor comprendido entre 20 y 25.

Con cierta frecuencia, la persona que quiere perder peso, por razones objetivas o no para hacerlo, comienza su intento de régimen dejando de lado el desayuno. Pero, a menudo, olvida o desconoce que en la persona obesa lo único que sobra es grasa. Es decir, que la restricción dietética debe recaer fundamentalmente sobre este macronutriente, siendo ésta la base de la reducción energética, puesto que una dieta hipocalórica bien planificada debe ser equilibrada en «todo lo demás».

Así pues, a la persona obesa le sobran reservas de grasas, pero no de azúcares; en consecuencia, y centrándonos en el desayuno, está tan necesitada de azúcares por la mañana como cualquier otro individuo. Es más, la dieta hipocalórica pretende evitar al máximo posible cualquier sufrimiento inútil, y por ello reparte las ingestas en cuatro o cinco tomas diarias en las que, naturalmente, no falta el desayuno.

Ésta y otras medidas drásticas olvidan, además, que el auténtico problema del exceso de peso es crónico y que, por consiguiente, las medidas que habrá que adoptar deberán ser seguidas durante mucho tiempo, si no toda la vida.

En definitiva, cuando realmente sea necesario perder peso, resultará una buena medida elegir para el desayuno lácteos desnatados, frutas con un contenido en azúcares medio-bajo y mantener un consumo moderado de cereales, evitando los alimentos superfluos. Y recordar que, a igualdad de peso, las tostadas son más calóricas que el pan tierno, pues han perdido agua al tostarlas y, contrariamente a lo que a veces se dice, ¡el agua no engorda!

## HIPERTENSIÓN

Existen algunas dificultades para definir cuáles son los límites de la normalidad de la hipertensión arterial, existiendo una gama de valores que va desde los universalmente aceptados como normales (120 / 80 mm Hg), a los unánimemente considerados como anormales (p. ej. 170 / 100 mm Hg). Para concretar, se adopta como límite superior de la tensión normal el valor de 140 / 90 mm Hg.

La hipertensión es un factor de riesgo primario de arteriosclerosis, y en la actualidad se admite que entre el 10 y el 20 % de la población adulta de los países industrializados es hipertensa. Del total de casos, el 85-90 % corresponde a la llamada hipertensión primaria o esencial, lo que equivale a decir que se desconocen los factores causales. Las causas involucradas en la génesis de la hipertensión son múltiples y entre ellas, además de la edad, la raza, el sexo y el estado de estrés, figuran, claro está, la obesidad y la ingesta excesiva de sal.

Dada la relación existente entre obesidad e hipertensión, uno de los planteamientos fundamentales de la dieta del hipertenso es la reducción del peso corporal cuando éste sea elevado.

La frecuente ingesta excesiva de sodio se debe al consumo elevado de sal (cloruro de sodio) que se añade en la cocina y en la mesa, y también en multitud de productos alimenticios industriales. Desde este punto de vista, el desayuno que incluye a los grupos de alimentos básicos recomendados deberá vigilar fundamentalmente dos alimentos: el pan y los quesos. La adición de sal al pan es excesiva y a ello se hizo referencia en el «Consenso para el control de la hipertensión arterial en España», donde los expertos recomendaron emprender las actuaciones necesarias para reducir la cantidad de sodio en el pan. Por su parte, los quesos, unos más que otros, son alimentos ricos en sodio; el requesón, con un contenido próximo a los 80 mg / 100 g, se situaría en el límite inferior de este tipo de alimentos. Por contra, los alimentos ricos en potasio, como las frutas frescas, pueden tener un efecto beneficioso sobre el control de la tensión arterial.

En definitiva, el desayuno para el hipertenso con un peso normal deberá seguir las reglas generales, considerando la adición de sodio al pan (posibilidad de utilizar pan sin sal) u otros productos derivados del trigo, y la riqueza en sodio de los quesos. En caso de que el hipertenso sea obeso, se añadirán a estos consejos los propuestos para la obesidad.

## COLESTEROL ELEVADO

El colesterol es un lípido fundamental para la vida. Ahora bien, cuando sus niveles se elevan por encima de lo normal, se convierte en un factor de riesgo primario de la arteriosclerosis. ¿Y cuáles son los valores considerados como normales? Hoy se admite que el riesgo de padecer una enfermedad cardiovascular aumenta a medida que lo hace el nivel de colesterol plasmático, especialmente cuando éste supera los 200 mg / dl, cifra que se aconseja no superar.

La relación entre alimentación y nivel de colesterol es estrecha. En este sentido, y en contra de lo que podría pensarse, el factor nutricional más importante no es el propio colesterol de la dieta, aunque ello no quiere decir que no deba controlarse, sino las grasas y, en particular, las grasas saturadas, de las que es necesario evitar un consumo excesivo. La dieta aterogénica se define como una dieta que presenta:

- Una ingesta excesiva de grasas saturadas y colesterol. Se aconseja que las primeras aporten como máximo un 10 % del VCT (valor calórico total) y el segundo un máximo de 300 mg / día.
- Una baja proporción de la relación grasas insaturadas / grasas saturadas. Lo más adecuado es que esta relación sea igual a dos o superior, a expensas principalmente de las grasas monoinsaturadas (ácido oleico).
- Un contenido bajo en fibra, cuya ingesta recomendada, como ya se ha indicado, oscila entre los 30 y los 35 g / día.

Cuando existen valores elevados de colesterol, se deben elegir los productos lácteos desnatados. En relación con el patrón de alimentos básicos indicado para el desayuno, ésta sería, con diferencia, la modificación más importante que se debería realizar. Por contra, el consumo de frutas y cereales está indicado en situaciones de hipercolesterolemia, pues contienen muy pocas grasas y aportan fibra.

Puesto que el consumo de alimentos tipo bollería va en aumento y la cantidad de grasas saturadas de los mismos suele ser elevada, deberá evitarse su consumo, o al menos, reducirse. Dado que uno de los principales colectivos consumidores de este tipo de productos son los niños y que, según señalan los expertos, su nivel de colesterol es elevado, existe un interés real en limitar su consumo, dentro del marco de una política de prevención.

En los envases de algunos productos de bollería podemos leer el mensaje «sin colesterol»; generalmente se trata de alimentos en los que no se ha utilizado para su elaboración huevo entero o su yema (en la clara no hay colesterol). Pero el «sin colesterol» de la etiqueta no quiere decir, como pueda pensar el consumidor incauto, que su ingestión no pueda ejercer una influencia negativa sobre nuestro colesterol plasmático, considerando el protagonismo que en ello tienen las grasas saturadas. Es el contenido en éstas, no siempre lo suficientemente bien especificado, el primer aspecto al que debemos prestar atención.

Otra «estrategia» comercial utilizada para la comercialización de este tipo de productos consiste en resaltar la presencia de grasas vegetales, con la esperanza de que el consumidor las asocie a grasas de «mejor calidad». No obstante, estamos otra vez ante una nueva trampa: las grasas de coco y palma, muy utilizadas en la elaboración de alimentos comerciales, presentan perfiles grasos similares o peores que las grasas animales; además, las grasas vegetales pueden haber sido más o menos hidrogenadas (saturadas), no presentando las mismas características nutricionales que las del producto original.

## ESTREÑIMIENTO

El estreñimiento afecta a una parte importante de la población. Si se define como dificultad para defecar, los afectados son un 20 %, mientras que esa cifra se reduce a un 5 % si se define como menos de dos deposiciones semanales. En general, puede aceptarse como ritmo defecatorio normal desde una deposición cada dos días a dos o tres deposiciones por día.

Su frecuencia aumenta con el paso de los años, por lo que su incidencia es mayor en los ancianos.

En el estreñimiento se produce un retraso en la velocidad del tránsito intestinal. El mantenimiento del volumen de la masa residual del colon es un factor primordial para provocar un peristaltismo eficaz y permitir así su avance hacia el recto. El estreñimiento puede deberse a múltiples causas no ligadas a la alimentación: sedentarismo, rigidez de horarios, inestabilidad emocional, ciertos fármacos, enfermedades intestinales...

Pero también los hábitos alimentarios incorrectos pueden facilitar su aparición. En este sentido, el factor clásico es la insuficiencia de fibra alimenticia en la dieta. Se ha comprobado que el aumento de la cantidad de fibra en la dieta se asocia a un mayor peso de las heces, a un aumento del número de deposiciones y a una disminución del tiempo de tránsito gastrointestinal.

Si bien no se ha demostrado que los pacientes estreñidos ingieren menos fibra que los no estreñidos, lo cierto es que muchos individuos estreñidos responden a dietas ricas en fibra (20-30 g / día), aunque no está claro en qué medida puede actuar como efecto placebo. La fibra de trigo es la que produce mayor incremento en el peso fecal, seguida de la de las frutas.

Puesto que la fibra sólo se encuentra en alimentos de origen vegetal, la dieta actual, rica en productos cárnicos, puede beneficiarse de una mayor presencia de cereales integrales, legumbres, frutas y hortalizas. El desayuno puede contribuir con frutas y cereales al aporte diario de fibra. No obstante, existe cierta polémica acerca de la posible interferencia del ácido fítico, presente en los cereales integrales, en la absorción del calcio.

Dentro del conjunto de medidas higiénico-dietéticas que se aconsejan frente al estreñimiento, figuran algunas tomas en ayunas: ciruelas secas puestas en remojo la noche anterior, un vaso de agua tibia, agua tibia con zumo de limón, una cucharada de aceite de oliva virgen en ayunas, un vaso de agua fría con sorbitol, e incluso un zumo de naranja...

Estos remedios, de mayor o menor eficacia según las características individuales y la causa del estreñimiento, pueden ser coadyuvantes, aunque en ningún caso suplen las recomendaciones dietéticas generales. Por supuesto, tampoco sustituyen al desayuno, y a la hora de valorar la relación entre beneficios y posibles perjuicios que presentan, hay que tener muy en cuenta cómo pueden afectar al desayuno normal.

## OSTEOPOROSIS

La osteoporosis es el resultado de un desequilibrio entre los procesos «programados» de síntesis (formación) y resorción (destrucción) del hueso, en favor de esta última, que puede producirse por múltiples factores, teniendo como consecuencia para el tejido una pérdida de masa ósea y una alteración de la microarquitectura del hueso, y como manifestación clínica la fractura: fémur, cadera, muñeca, vértebras...

Una de las características principales de estas fracturas es que se producen por impactos mínimos, conociéndose como fracturas «espontáneas». Las características hormonales de la mujer la hacen particularmente sensible a este trastorno, en especial tras la menopausia: una mujer puede perder durante los cinco primeros años de menopausia (que es una etapa fisiológica y no una enfermedad) el 15 % de la masa ósea. A ello hay que añadir la pérdida de masa ósea propia de la edad, que se produce en ambos sexos.

Evidentemente, la mejor forma de hacer frente a la osteoporosis es la prevención, es decir, favoreciendo el máximo potencial de crecimiento óseo durante las tres primeras décadas de la vida y creando las condiciones más favorables para el posterior mantenimiento de una buena masa ósea. El ejercicio, el mantenimiento de un peso corporal adecuado y una dieta equilibrada son tres factores fundamentales para ello.

En relación con la dieta, hoy está admitido que una ingesta adecuada de calcio durante todo el período vital es esencial para el desarrollo y mantenimiento del esqueleto. Y para nosotros, la fuente alimenticia principal de calcio son los alimentos lácteos, sin cuya presencia será muy difícil alcanzar las cifras que de este elemento se recomiendan a cualquier edad.

Por su parte, cereales y frutas son fuentes poco significativas de este elemento, si bien frutas como higos, naranjas, mandarinas, nísperos y chirimoyas, con sus 30-40 mg / 100 g, pueden aportar cantidades considerables. Además, las frutas son una de las mejores fuentes de vitamina C, un nutriente necesario para la formación del colágeno, una proteína fundamental de la matriz orgánica del hueso, que representa, aproximadamente, del 35 al 40 % del mismo.

# PROPUESTAS SUGERENTES, VARIADAS, NUTRITIVAS Y SALUDABLES PARA DESAYUNAR

La monotonía es uno de los enemigos de un buen desayuno. Pero, en realidad, las propuestas actuales dejan un margen extremadamente amplio en el que caben numerosas posibilidades; combinaciones nutritivas y sabrosas que pueden, en días especiales, ser aún superadas.

El desayuno se convierte así en un ejemplo de que el buen comer y el comer bien no tienen por qué estar disociados, tal y como muy frecuentemente lo entiende un amplio sector de la población. Y es que el hecho de que la gastronomía vaya de la mano de la dietética es, mucho más de lo que parece, tan sólo una cuestión de inteligencia. Por contra, los estereotipos, las rigideces y las fragmentaciones se empeñan en mantener polaridades enfrentadas. Puesto que somos nosotros mismos los que pensamos nuestra comida, haremos bien en esforzarnos por obtener el máximo placer de nuestras necesidades.

A la hora de decidir qué es lo que vamos a desayunar, puede resultar de interés tener presente algunas consideraciones generales:

- Las recomendaciones no son reglas fijas, sino puntos de referencia. El riesgo de desequilibrios aumenta en la medida en que nos alejamos de ellas, tanto por exceso como por defecto.

- De los alimentos habitualmente propuestos para un buen desayuno, sólo las frutas están sometidas a ritmos estacionales. Para los demás alimentos, las estaciones sólo pueden influir en cuanto a volumen, temperatura...
- En algunas preparaciones podemos obtener ventaja empezando los preparativos la noche anterior. Para otras muchas, la inmediatez de la preparación es una garantía de valor nutricional e higiénico.
- Desde el punto de vista de la conservación, las frutas y los lácteos son los alimentos más sensibles. Por consiguiente serán ellos los que definirán cuáles son los criterios de compra y consumo más apropiados. En este sentido, una planificación semanal de los desayunos será de gran utilidad.
- Los batidos no deben ser nunca una estrategia para acabar con frutas que no están en condiciones. Por contra, sí pueden ser una buena solución para el consumo de piezas de aspecto poco agraciado.

## PROPUESTAS

Presentamos a continuación 40 propuestas que pretenden cubrir un amplio abanico de gustos, situaciones, necesidades y posibilidades. Evidentemente, cualquiera de ellas es convertible en función de cada caso. Interesa siempre acercarse lo más posible a la trilogía alimentaria básica. Para aquellas propuestas marcadas con un asterisco, remitimos al lector a la sección «Recetas» que aparece tras las propuestas. Las cantidades de cada alimento hacen referencia, en principio, a lo que en el apartado «El mejor desayuno» se define como ración, aunque, naturalmente, se adaptarán a las necesidades individuales.

1. • pera
   • tostadas con requesón y miel

2. • palosanto (caqui)
   • cuajada con miel
   • palitos de sésamo

3. • uvas
   • pan con queso

4. • yogur con piña troceada
   • galletas

5. • fresas con chocolate
   • bizcocho

6. • yogur con granada
   • pan dextrinado

7. • zumo de manzana
   • pan con tomate y tortilla

8. • zumo de piña
   • pan de higo con queso tierno

9. • sopa de sandía*

10. • chirimoyas
    • galletas de arroz con halva*
    • yogur líquido

11. • zumo de mandarina
    • yogur con gofio de maíz, miel y dátiles

12. • kiwi
    • yogur con muesli

13. • manzana rallada con nata
      líquida (1 cucharada) y pasas
    • coca de horno

14. • cerezas
    • tarta de queso

15. • tortilla de manzana
    • pan de centeno

16. • higos con queso fresco de oveja
    • horchata de chufa con miel y tropezones
      de pan

17. • batido de leche y fruta
    • barquillos

18. • zumo de naranja
    • tostadas con queso fresco y dulce
      de membrillo

19. • barca de melón*

20. • albaricoques
    • leche con cereales

21. • manzana al horno
    • tostadas con queso de cabra y mermelada
      de frambuesa

22. • mandarinas
    • castañas con requesón*

23. • papaya con yogur
    • plumcake

24. • batido de plátano con yogur

25. • zumo de naranja
    • huevo pasado por agua
    • bastones de pan integral

26. • ciruelas
    • copos de avena con kéfir y miel

27. • yogur líquido
    • tarta de manzana

28. • zumo de uva
    • brioches con pasta de chocolate

29. • zumo de manzana y piña
    • crepes de pasta de avellana*
    • leche

30. • melocotón
    • tostadas con miel y mantequilla

31. • pera al horno
    • arroz con leche

32. • cerezas
    • tartaletas de tres quesos al horno*

33. • macedonia de frutas
    • natillas
    • galletas de arroz

34. • flan con pera al horno
    • tostadas

35. • zumo de granada
    • sándwich caliente de queso

36. • ciruelas
    • tofu con miel
    • pan integral de centeno

37. • zumo de pomelo
    • coca de cabello de ángel
    • queso quark

38. • higos
    • crema de calabaza (con leche) con sirope
      de manzana

39. • zumo de mandarina
    • «leche de soja» con miel
    • cereales de desayuno

40. • batido de piña con yogur
    • bastoncillos

# RECETAS

## Sopa de sandía

*Ingredientes por ración:*
- 150 g de sandía (desprovista de la piel)
- una cucharada de miel
- un vaso de yogur o cualquier otra leche fermentada
- cinco o seis dátiles deshuesados
- tres rebanadas de pan dextrinado
- una cucharada de nata líquida (opcional)

*Preparación:*
Pasar la sandía por la licuadora. Añadir la miel, el yogur y, en caso de utilizarse, la nata. Remover bien. Incorporar los dátiles y el pan dextrinado en forma de tropezones.

## Halva

*Ingredientes para 4 personas:*
- 60 g de sésamo
- 60 g de miel

*Preparación:*
Batir el sésamo hasta conseguir un polvo fino (un molinillo resulta ideal). Colocar en un bol, añadir la miel y remover hasta conseguir una pasta homogénea.

## Barca de melón

*Ingredientes para una persona:*
- $^1/_2$ melón de tamaño pequeño
- un melocotón
- un vaso de yogur o kéfir
- una cucharada de melaza
- dos pizcas de canela en polvo

*Preparación:*
Una vez partido el melón, retirar las semillas de su interior. Añadir en su lugar el melocotón cortado a trocitos. Verter ahora el vaso de yogur o kéfir. Extender por encima la melaza y, finalmente, espolvorear la canela.

## Castañas con requesón

*Ingredientes para dos personas:*
- 150 g de castañas tostadas y peladas
- 200 g de requesón
- dos cucharadas de miel
- el zumo de dos limones

*Preparación:*
Disponer las castañas en un plato hondo. Incorporar el requesón cortado a dados. Batir la miel con el zumo de limón y rociar.

## Crepes de pasta de avellana

*Ingredientes para la masa de ocho a diez crepes:*
- 275 ml de leche
- un huevo
- una cucharadita de aceite de girasol
- 110 g de harina de trigo (puede ser integral)
- una pizca de sal

*Preparación:*
Mezclar la leche, el huevo y el aceite en la batidora hasta formar una masa homogénea. Agregar la harina y la sal, y volver a mezclar. Si es posible, dejar reposar la mezcla durante 30 minutos. Volver a mezclar. Para elaborar cada crepe, colocar en una sartén caliente, untada con un poco de aceite, dos cucharadas soperas de la masa. A continuación, dis-

tribuir bien la mezcla por toda la superficie. Reducir un poco el fuego y cocinar de uno a dos minutos por cada lado.

*Ingredientes para la pasta de avellana, por crepe:*
- 30 g de avellanas
- 10 g de miel líquida
- una cucharada de nata líquida

*Preparación:*
Batir las avellanas hasta reducirlas a polvo. Colocar en un bol, y añadir la miel y la nata. Remover bien hasta conseguir una masa homogénea.

## Tartaletas de tres quesos al horno

*Ingredientes por tartaleta:*
- 20 g de Emmental
- 30 g de Cottage
- 10 g de Roquefort

*Preparación:*
Mezclar el Cottage con el Roquefort y colocar en la tartaleta. Poner por encima una loncha de Emmental. Hornear.

Las tartaletas, ya elaboradas, se pueden adquirir en los establecimientos de productos dietéticos.

# BIBLIOGRAFÍA

DUPIN H., CUQ J. L., MALEWIAK M. I., LEYNAUD-ROUAUD C., BERTHIER A. M. *La alimentación humana*. Ed. Bellaterra. 1997.

Fundación Española de la Nutrición. *Problemática del desayuno en la nutrición de los españoles*. Publ. Serie Divulgación, nº 3.

MATAIX J., CARAZO E. *Nutrición para educadores*. Ed. Díaz de Santos. 1995.

Ministerio de Sanidad y Consumo. *Tablas de composición de alimentos españoles*. 1995

MOREIRAS O., CARBAJAL A., CABRERA Mª. L. *La composición de los alimentos*. Eudema Universidad. 1992.

Generalitat de Catalunya. *Protocols dietètics per a l´atenció primària*. 1992.

National Research Council. *Recommended Dietary Allowances (R.D.A.) 1ª edición española de la 10ª edición original*. Ed. Consulta. 1991.

SERRA LL., ARANCETA J., MATAIX J. *Guías alimentarias para la población española. Documento de Consenso*. S. G. Editores. 1995.

SERRA LL., ARANCETA J., MATAIX J. *Nutrición y Salud Pública: métodos, bases científicas y aplicaciones*. Ed. Masson. 1995.

11783822R00106

SUSAN BADARACCO

# DANCE WITH ME

*My words are an inadequate tribute to my mother who will remain in my heart forever.*

*The Present*

The dance floor, a small empty space between her bed and bathroom, was sticky with the residue of an industrial cleaner. Mom clutched a plaid pillow to her chest and took ragged, deep breaths from her huddled position on top of the bed. Food splatters stained her shield and in the past she would've shared my revulsion at holding the lumpy object so close to her face. Now we're both grateful anytime she can find something to hold on to. Her stark eyes darted around the room, skirting past the photograph of a man who smiled benignly from a tarnished metal frame and landing instead on a buff colored stuffed puppy—the later provided more comfort to her when she could hear noises outside her room that unnerved her. Her fingers, with nails that were torn and grimy, incessantly tugged on the loose threads of her pastel quilt, a bed covering battered by its repeated washings.

"Come on, you know you want to do it," my sister coaxed.

Mom closed her eyes, but one side of her mouth twitched.

My sister's eyes sparkled with merriment. She's a better faker than I am, I get heartsick when I see her like this. She tugged Mom's arm until Mom nodded and slid her feet to the floor. Mom stumbled, then shuffled to the center of the room, the pillow still crushed against her chest. Her lips remained tightly compressed and her eyes wary, but she accepted the invitation. That didn't always happen.

"I Say a Little Prayer" by Aretha Franklin streamed from the CD player on her dresser. Mom blinked at the familiarity of the tune and a smile touched her lips. My sister sensed victory, grinned back at her, and then raised Mom's hand up with a flourish. "Dance with me," she urged.

Mom swayed her hips. The pillow slipped to the floor and my sister used a foot to slide it out of the way. Mom twirled in a circle, ducking under the hand that still held her own. Her voice croaked out words, mostly made-up, but the tune was at least reminiscent of the one playing.

As the song progressed, her movements became more dramatic. She released her hold on my sister's hand and focused on the music. Scooted back and forth and then sashayed several steps to the left, pivoting and flinging her arms out dramatically while scanning the room to make sure her audience was watching. She shimmied her shoulders, not in rhythm with the music, but with confidence nonetheless. Her slippered feet explored the floor, tapping, sliding and twirling. A childlike giddiness replaced the desolation in her eyes, and it was as if, for 3.09 minutes, the heavy weight of her diagnosis was stripped from her slender shoulders. She was free, unfettered from the fogginess, distrust and paranoia that stalked her relentlessly.

*The Prelude*

randma was a miniature bulldozer with a sharp tongue and the unwavering belief that she knew what was best for everyone. Grandpa tolerated her. Grandpa's personality and build was that of a long-distance runner, laid back and lanky. It wasn't unusual for him to pop out of the chair where he'd been reading his crime drama, position his head on a pillow, and kick up his feet. His sinewy legs might flail momentarily, but eventually they would settle into their lean against the wall and he would grin at me, upside down, in his headstand.

A growing pile of coins on his dresser signaled something was amiss. When he found himself unable to calculate the correct sum, Grandpa settled on handing dollar bills to cashiers and pocketing the change.

Grandma was a staunch Catholic and once taught two cats to bow their heads in prayer prior to their evening meal.

I have a cat and it's the most headstrong animal I've encountered. Tass walks down the length of my counters like it's her personal catwalk, despite swats and sprays of water. When Grandma was on a mission, there was no option for failure. She thought teaching her husband forgotten math concepts was just a matter of buying a used arithmetic book. They worked at the kitchen table, his sparse hair falling over his forehead, his pencil pushing too hard into the page.

Grandma did her best to be patient. But the longer they worked, the higher her voice went up. She'd frown, scrub away the incorrect answers with a pink eraser and then start again. "Now, Joe, you know what seven and three is…" Afterward she'd sit alone on a stool in the kitchen, blowing cigarette smoke through pursed lips while she stared at a blank wall.

The math book disappeared when Grandpa was officially diagnosed with Alzheimer's. They stopped going to the library for his crime books when she realized that he didn't remember what he'd read earlier that same day. She kept the car keys in her purse and when he asked to drive, she insisted that it wasn't his turn.

Once a week, my mom took Grandpa to her house to give Grandma a break from the relentless task of guiding, supervising, and manipulating him. Mom would look for minor tasks to keep him occupied, wiping the kitchen counters or dusting the bookcase. When she assigned him the duty of cleaning the front door, he rubbed his cloth in a steady diagonal motion, ignoring the specks of glass cleaner on either side. "Don't worry about it." Mom's face softened when I pointed out the marks he'd left behind. I was itching to take over his job, to eliminate those flecks, and restore the door to its sparkling original state. But Mom was no longer concerned about the things that don't really matter.

Mom focused exclusively on her family, watching over

not only her father, but also babysitting for my toddler on weekends. When I returned from one errand, Grandpa and my three-year-old daughter were outside, sweeping the back porch where baskets of pink and tangerine portulaca swayed in a breeze smelling of cut grass. Grandpa had my mother's old kitchen broom and my daughter worked with a pink toy version. Neither of them noticed my arrival. My grandpa paused his sweeping when he heard a noise from the yard. He leaned his broom against the brick wall and set out to investigate the crape myrtle whose limbs shifted and rustled. He yelped when the sparrow burst from the shrub, threw his hands over his face, and made a hasty retreat to the porch.

Without slowing, he strode toward my daughter, intent on removing her broom in order to resume his task. But she wasn't interested in giving up her toy, and her delicate face flushed red in the tug-of-war that ensued. She blistered him with a scowl, stomped her feet in rebellion, and when that didn't work, she opened up her mouth and released a screech of outrage that spoke of the unfairness of her situation and came close to rupturing my eardrums. Unfazed, he carried away his prize.

Struck by the absurdity of what I'd witnessed, I was slow to respond to my own daughter's cry. My mom flew out the screen door, assessed the situation, replaced the appropriate brooms to their owners, and restored order. There is a reverse movement in the Alzheimer's clock, it's not just about forgotten names and experiences. It's a backward march of maturity.

Taking care of Grandpa became increasingly difficult for Grandma. He needed help dressing, would get frustrated, and even angry, if Grandma make him change from clothing inappropriate for the season. He relentlessly paced the length of their small home when he lost the ability to read and the television held no interest for him. Cooking on the stove

became impossible for Grandma. Fascinated by the way the burners transformed from black to glowing red, he'd reach out his hand, and she'd swat it away. He left the house for spontaneous walks, sometimes when her head was halfway in the dryer pulling out an errant sock...other times in the middle of the night when the click of the door closing was her only warning he'd slipped away. Grandma's already lined face looked haggard.

When they moved into an assisted living center, it was someone else's responsibility to cook and remember to pay the electric bill. They socialized with other residents and went on excursions to see wild flowers and local theater productions. But when he forgot to use a fork and could no longer take part in simple conversations, Grandma's world shrunk into the size of their one-bedroom apartment.

She didn't have time to grieve for the lost friendships. She had to focus on installing door latches that Grandpa couldn't operate, to find bribes that would entice my previously meticulous grandfather to climb into a stall where the water erupted from the wall without warning. He scrambled away from the assault, blinking his eyes from the burn of the shampoo and slipping, careening, on the linoleum floor. Grandma learned to put a towel on the recliner he lurched toward. He stared at his bony knees with his shoulders stooped and the tendons of his neck taut. His jaw clenched, unclenched, in time with the shaking of his fisted hands. Unperturbed, Grandma blotted the water from his chest, used a wet washcloth to remove the residual shampoo, all the while, chiding him for what was an "uncalled-for, ridiculous reaction to a bit of warm water". He refused to look at her.

Grandma distracted him at the dinner table, working to get a few spoonfuls in his mouth before he lost interest. She scoured the apartment for potential threats to a confused

man. Grandma and Mom would brainstorm solutions to every problem. But, eventually, they ran out of answers.

By their very nature, these facilities (nursing homes, convalescent homes, assisted living centers, rest homes) are a disappointment. Families would like to believe they are moving their loved one to an environment where the care is better than they can provide at home. In reality, when you sign that contract, it feels like you're waving the white flag of defeat. Grandma was unable to keep up with the *Alice in Wonderland* world my Grandpa functioned within. Her life had no rules or routines because his didn't.

She cried the day they moved him into his room. A strong, some would say stubborn woman, this broke my grandma. They'd married young and had their first baby, my mom, during the period of the Great Depression. Despite my grandpa's trepidation at supporting his new family when money was scarce, they survived and added a son. As with most couples, they had good years and bad. In the photographs of their fiftieth wedding anniversary, Grandpa smiled, but his eyes looked unfocused. Grandma looked like she was in the middle of instructing him about something, which was likely. It would be their last anniversary together. Grandma might've wept when they moved him into his new residence, but she slept, uninterrupted, for the first time in months.

Mom and Grandma muttered about his laundry, the cleanliness of the bathroom, and a host of other small details they felt the staff neglected. While they took turns tidying up his room and washing his clothes to their satisfaction, Grandpa stopped eating.

Alzheimer's provides more questions than answers. What controls whether it will be a good day or a bad day? What triggers an anger outburst? The paranoia? Does nothing

work to help sleep? *Did my grandfather stop eating and drinking on purpose?*

The average person dies between three and ten days once they stop drinking water. Grandpa had only been in his new home a few weeks when an aide recognized what was going on. First he refused his food, then his water. She informed my mom and grandma that Grandpa was dying. When most people lie in bed, it's from an injury, illness or surgery. It's considered a temporary setback, requiring an indeterminate period of time for recovery, and then everything returns to normal again. When my mom told me what the aide said, I could hear the disbelief in her voice.

I'm a pediatrician and, by habit, I started doing a visual examination as soon as I reached his bedside. When you're in the medical field, you make assessments on skin color, respirations, and level of consciousness, before you lay hands on someone. I touched his veined hand, the slender fingers that once curled around mine as he instructed me on the right grip of a tennis racket. "Do something," my mother pleaded. The aide placed an oxygen cannula under his nose, murmured comments about keeping him comfortable and tucked in his sheets. I did nothing.

My mom was impatient with my silence. Her grip left white finger marks on my arm when she tugged me aside, begging me to arrange his transfer to a hospital. "Save him," she insisted. I don't recall what I said to her. I was flustered and thought I'd come to say goodbye to my grandpa, not resuscitate him. As I bent over the bedside railing, my mother paced behind me, still pleading. I wasn't used to hearing my mother ask for anything and I dreaded giving my response. Grandma was uncharacteristically quiet.

Grandpa's lips were dry and cracked. His once craggy face looked skeletal with sunken eyes and hollowed cheeks. I reached for a wet washcloth, dabbed it on his lips, and tried

to squeeze a bit of moisture in his mouth. His eyes popped opened and met mine. For months, my grandpa's eyes were unfocused, empty of any recognition of his surroundings. The grandpa I knew vacated his gaunt frame. But in that moment, he said two words that proved he was lucid.

"Susan, no."

I withdrew, shocked that he would remember my name and in obedience to the grandpa I loved and respected. Mom and Grandma didn't hear him, they were too preoccupied coming up with a plan to pull him back from the precipice he walked along. But I heard him.

An odd thing about Alzheimer's is the brief moments when the neurons in the brain connect and function as they were designed to. This random action allows recognition of faces, emergence of random memories, and possibly, a recognition of their situation. I had a glimpse of the grandfather I thought I'd left behind and with those two words, I knew that my grandpa was ready to die. I imagine he craved it. I explained to my mother and grandmother that there would be no transfer to a hospital, no IV fluids, or any other heroic measures. Nothing would be done to stop the inevitable. The aide echoed my words and repeated her promise to keep him comfortable.

I don't know what it feels like to die of dehydration. The dry, sticky mouth. The relentless desire for fluids. I never thought about how the urine concentrates in the body's desperate attempt to hold on to liquids. My mom and I took my grandpa to the toilet when he refused, or didn't understand how to use a bedside container. We stood on either side of him, supporting his weak body over the commode. When he finally released the stream, he closed his eyes, his emaciated body quaked, and he released a long drawn-out moan.

I imagine the uric acid crystals, formed in the sludge that

was all his body would release in place of his normal urine, burned his urethra as he peed. My mom and I held him upright, kept him from collapsing onto the linoleum floor. Mom kept up a litany of apologies the entire time— lamenting that I should see him undressed, should have to clean up the liquid that dribbled from his bottom.

What goes on in people's heads when they take over the most elemental tasks of caring for another human? I can't speak for everyone. For me, the intimacy gives me a profound sense of privilege that another person trusts me to this level. I have a sense of rightness about where I am and what I'm doing. I reassured my mother and we finished our task.

Grandpa relaxed after we brought him back to bed, no longer writhing or getting his legs twisted in the sheets. I assumed he was more comfortable after going to the bathroom, but the aide recognized the signs. "It's almost time". I reached for my grandpa's hand, inched my fingers toward his wrist so I could feel his pulse. My grandma knew what I was doing, for years she worked as a medical assistant. She watched my face, and I nodded to her when I felt the tapping under my finger.

Within moments though, it disappeared.

I was certain that I'd shifted my fingers without being aware, somehow slid off the correct spot in his bony wrist. I searched his crepey skin for those slight pulsations that indicated his heart was still pumping and then moved my hand to his carotid, a larger vessel in his neck, when I couldn't locate his pulse. I was relieved when I felt the subtle beats within the corded tendons of his neck. But a few taps later and these, too, disappeared.

I leaned back, overcome by what had just happened. I was touching my grandpa the very moment when his life came to an end. In contrast to what I'd often witnessed in the hospi-

tal, his death was quiet. No frantic orders. No torn packages of needles and gauze. No beeping monitors or defibrillators. My grandma suspected something had happened, but needed confirmation. Her words came out agitated and strident, "IS HE DEAD?"

The aide moved closer to the head of the bed and positioned her fingers as I had done. She concentrated for a moment and then, without turning, she answered my grandma. "Your husband's at peace now." My grandma sagged over the bed with the bedsheets still clutched in her hands. When she finally spoke, her voice was low and fervent.

"Thank God... I thought he'd died."

Grandma looked baffled when I explained he was gone.

~

ALZHEIMER'S DISEASE is a roller coaster whose route changes daily. A game of hide and seek involving memories and abilities. It unleashes a bewildering quagmire of emotions.

Watching my grandpa struggle with Alzheimer's was my first real encounter with the disease. My mom and grandma taught me what a difficult honor it is to be a caretaker of a victim. An impossible task, really. I saw my grandma's sorrow and disbelief when my grandpa died, but I also recognized that a burden had been lifted.

3

---

*Where words leave off, music begins.*
— Heinrich Heine

*M*aya was a rescue chihuahua with an attitude. Scrappy and underweight, she had large brown eyes and a deformed spine. When she bent her head to eat, her back legs rose from the ground, leaving her in an odd tripod position. I'd never seen anything like her. The cooked chicken Mom fed her helped her gain weight, and she kept her legs earthbound like a decent animal, but she held dog food in disdain afterward. She'd stare at you with an accusatory expression and she'd go on hunger strikes until someone broke down and gave her something entirely inappropriate. Like a fast food burger.

Mom allowed this prima donna of a dog to decide the direction of our walks and how long to stop for sniffs and pees. With perked ears and an upright tail, Maya pranced as she walked. That is, when she walked. Mom would pick her

up to avoid muddy spots or crushed acorn shells that might scratch her paws. Maya spent most of her existence in the folds of my mom's arms.

It had been almost twenty years since Grandpa's death. Fall leaves drifted onto the sidewalk, and the morning was cool enough to warrant a sweater over our tee-shirts. Mom and I chatted about the neighbor's new door color and my son's orthodontic appointment. We stopped, started again, based on the dog's itinerary. In the midst of relating some family drama, I failed to notice that my mother was no longer at my side.

Maya flew past me and Mom was just a leash length behind. Her short hair bounced with each stride, and her size five sneakers pelted the sidewalk. I spun around, ready to confront any human or animal threatening my mom, but there was nothing there. It was a bizarre comedy. I caught up with Mom, and using more strength than you would think to pull back an almost ten pound dog, extracted the leash from her hands. Mom had a history of osteoporosis, was sixty-eight-years old, and never broke a sweat in any activity she pursued. So what prompted the sprint?

"Maya wanted the squirrel," she explained.

~

DID Mom wonder about her chances of getting Alzheimer's? Did she worry about it? Did she question whether she was destined to follow her father's path? And when do we lose that feeling of invulnerability we have as a youth and recognize that all of us are at risk?

Mom, like her father, took part in an Alzheimer's study at the nearby medical school. She had no symptoms; they performed her testing to trend family members. She relayed several incidents regarding both of their evaluations.

13

Grandpa was given a mental status exam, a test that helps researchers and doctors document a patient's memory, judgement and ability to understand abstract thought. It starts easy. What is the year? The day of the week? It requires you to count backward from 100 by sevens. To follow directions: "Take the paper in your right hand, fold it in half, and put it on the floor." It also asks you to remember three objects. For instance: the color red, an apple, and a table.

The problem with this particular evaluation is that a lot of doctors use the exact same objects. They learned the test in medical school, memorized the components for simplicity, and never varied from it. My grandma listened, and for weeks after his exam she would ask him to remember those same three words—the color red, an apple, and a table. She effectively switched the items from his short-term memory into his long-term memory. He answered all three items correctly on his next test, but it turned out to be an insignificant victory.

They asked my mother a judgement question during her examination. "If you were lost in the woods, what would you do?" I'm sure several answers are acceptable. Locate a river and follow it out of the woods. Use the position of the sun to get your bearings. Tie ripped pieces of cloth around tree limbs to keep from walking in circles.

"I would sit down," Mom answered. I'm sure that caused a pause, maybe even a chin rub. After all, she was not diagnosed with Alzheimer's, she was the daughter of the study patient. "Why would you do that?" they questioned. Her answer didn't surprise me. "I've never had a good sense of direction and my family knows that I could not possibly get out of the woods by myself. I would stay in one place to make is easier for them to find me." Despite her confidence in us, over the coming years it grew harder and harder for us to find her.

~

RETURNED CHECKS FROM THE GAS, electric and phone company alerted Dad something was going on. Dad called me when he saw the odd numbers she'd written, bearing no relationship to the billed amounts. She was forgetting things —how to screw on the mayonnaise lid, where she kept the extra toilet paper and, most concerning of all, what time Sunday mass was held. I suspected the diagnosis when I made an appointment with a neurologist.

The waiting room's muted colors and design reminded me of someone's great aunt's living room. A damask sofa and love seat surrounded an oval mahogany coffee table with stacks of *Redbook*, *Good Housekeeping* and *Time* magazines. Scented frosted glass, looking exactly like the glass candy my aunt used to send each Christmas, filled a small crystal bowl next to silk flower arrangement with a thin layer of dust. I learned to move the bowl to keep Mom from putting the glass in her mouth.

I tried to distract her with small talk when the medical assistant took her vital signs and weight, wanting to shield my mother from what lay ahead. Afterward, we sat side by side in simple wooden chairs. Compared to the waiting room, the exam rooms were strictly functional. An exam table, cabinets with a plethora of medical items, an otoscope, and an unframed poster describing the signs of a stroke.

Mom went through the motions of turning pages, but none of the articles on fall fashion trends or illicit office romances held her interest. I rested one of my hands on her wrist, felt her shudder each time a chair scraped or a door shut somewhere beyond our tiny room. I'd entered the office in protective mode, but with each of her tremors, the feelings intensified until I wanted to rise up and do battle with some-thing…anything.

The neurologist was a petite woman with kind eyes and the ability to move fast in high heels. In the entire time we remained her patient, she'd never walk into a room—she burst through the door. Mom outlined her concerns, explained about her father and his diagnosis, and I reluctantly added a few of my own observations: the confusion driving to the grocery store where she'd shopped for the last two decades, the food forgotten in the oven, the need to look up phone numbers that used to be engraved in her memory. She documented each of our worries in her laptop, tapping the keys and stripping away our option to pretend her memory slips were normal.

The physical exam was brief, a glance at her open mouth, a peer into her ears, a cold stethoscope pressed against her chest. The questions, the mental status exam, came next. I leaned forward in my chair, touching her arm to remind her I was by her side. Despite looking worried, she did well on most of the questions. But then we hit a snag.

The neurologist asked mom to draw a clock and told her what time the hands should read. The 'clock test' is to screen for cognitive impairment. It requires understanding the instructions, being able to replicate a clock and recognizing where the clock hands should be positioned.

Mom drew a simple circle, but then she stalled. I chewed on my lips and waited for Mom to add numbers and hands to her drawing, but she couldn't put her pen back on the paper. The neurologist pointed to the clock on the wall. Clearly, this was "cheating" and I was split between relief for her assistance, and my concern about the validity of the results.

Mom copied the numbers wrong. When instructed to show "ten past eleven", she used a single clock hand curved to include both numbers. There are different scoring

systems for this test, but the easiest to remember is that if you don't complete the test correctly, you get a "0".

The neurologist wasn't finished—it was as if she didn't trust her own test. She asked Mom to look at the clock again. This time, instead of drawing it, she asked Mom to tell her what time it was. My hands tightened on the armrests. What was she doing? Surely, she could see that my mom did not understand the test. Mom grew flustered and made wild guesses. "Is it two o'clock? Five o'clock?"

The neurologist shook her head, gave us a bleak smile, and then left the room. Mom's shoulders sagged, and my stomach felt hollow. I tried hustling her out the door, but the medical assistant stopped us in the middle of our escape to schedule more testing.

MRI scans are one of the imaging studies for Alzheimer's. Shrinking of different areas of the brain is a common finding in Alzheimer's, but there's a lot of variability. Mom's scan didn't show any tumor or trauma explaining her memory problems. She had some atrophy, or shrinkage, but up to ninety-five percent of elderly adults have the same finding. The information wasn't helpful.

The neuropsychological testing took several hours and left mom exhausted. She didn't talk much afterwards, but took my hand like it was her lifeline. She had a wane, defeated look and I figured that sometime during the testing, she crossed the line from being worried about the Alzheimer's diagnosis to confronting her new reality.

I did my best to divert her with a lighthearted story about my son, but in the back of my mind I questioned why we put her through the testing in the first place. Was it important to validate what we already knew? I'd always put in my faith in medicine and still believed that there were answers, or at least pathways with predetermined stages and explanations on how to address the expected decline. I was naïve.

The testing did not lead to any ground-breaking management decisions. After I read the report, the physician side of me wanted to argue specific points about the diagnostic conclusion; the daughter side wanted to weep and throw my body over hers to protect her from the words that flew like shards of glass, leaving cuts that never quite healed.

Mom was in the early stages of Alzheimer's and she knew it. Her depression about the diagnosis didn't surprise me, I was despondent too. The neurologist recommended starting an antidepressant, reminded me that depression would cloud her thinking, and she didn't need that burden on top of the inevitable decline. Months later, when no one saw any difference, Mom stopped the medicine and outlined her plan—she didn't want to be a burden to us and insisted we place her in a memory center when the time was right.

Over time, Mom came to a certain peace with her diagnosis. I did not. I spent the first several years convinced the situation was a cosmic error, defying all definitions of karma. Mom volunteered to clean the public restrooms of her Catholic church ahead of important events. When the neighbor suffered a broken hip, mom took groceries to her house for weeks, ignoring the pungent urine smells of more than a dozen cats. She gave to charities, made care packages for soldiers, and hand wrote letters on the occasion of any wedding/birthday/illness. In short, my mom was a saint.

I waited for God to recognize his error. I know how crazy that sounds—I've taken care of children in a cancer ward. Admittedly, God should have taken steps to protect those little ones before concentrating on the disease attacking my mom. But there is a stage of denial when facing a painful diagnosis, and apparently, I'm not immune.

I never doubted God's presence in those days, but I never felt like he carried me over the troubled waters either. I started out the fired-up athlete pointing out an obvious foul

to an impassive-faced referee. His implacable silence troubled me and I wanted to be pulled from the game.

Medicine, my more tangible god, failed me too. I trusted I could find an answer to every question and a solution to every problem. I understood no cure existed, but surely therapeutic programs existed, medicines could be prescribed, specialists consulted. I'd underestimated Alzheimer's.

Hippocrates said our responsibility as physicians was to "cure sometimes, treat often, and comfort always". When I comforted families in the past, it almost felt like I was stepping out of my role as a doctor. Now I realize just how integral, how *fundamental*, the act of comforting is. Protecting, supporting and consoling my mom became more critical than anything medicine offered us.

4

---

*The journey between who you once were, and who you are now becoming, is where the dance of life really takes place.* —Barbara De Angelis

*D*ad wasn't the kind of guy to call me and inquire about my day. If he called, it meant they had a problem. He always started the conversation by asking about my job or the kids, but we both knew where it was going.

"SHE'S GETTING MORE CONFUSED."

"What happened?"

"She couldn't find the refrigerator."

*My mind spun, and I didn't know what to say. I asked, "What did you do?"*

*"I waited a while and then pointed it out to her. I told her, 'Look, Judy, I found it'. She felt better after that."*

· · ·

ON ANOTHER DAY:

*"Your Mom's had a bad morning."*

*"What happened?"*

*He was silent for a moment, and I could hear nothing but his slow breaths on the line.*

*"She's just extra confused today. Not doing well. Are you coming over?"*

THEY NEEDED foundation work on the house, and the workers pulled back the carpet and rearranged the furniture to get to the concrete underneath. Plastic drapes hung over every entrance into the den, protecting the rest of the rooms from dust, but also transforming the home into a carnival not-so-fun house. You could not reach a bedroom, a bathroom, or the kitchen without encountering an obstacle. It was disorienting for anyone; it was far worse for Mom.

I didn't argue with my parents, I might have tried debating with my mom about my curfew, but never my dad. His anger scared me. His eyes would harden, he'd stare at me with compressed lips until I flinched and backed down. But that day, I wasn't backing down.

"Why didn't you call me?" A reasonable question. But I wasn't acting reasonable. I was indignant, and reprimanded my father. "Didn't you think about how this would affect her? I would have arranged for her to stay with me for a few days."

His reaction was far worse than I expected. Instead of outrage, he looked resigned. Defeated. Old. He leaned back in his chair, met my eyes for only a moment, and then switched his gaze to something in the back yard. I left him

like that, staring into nothingness, and took my mom away. Someday, I might forgive myself for how I acted, but it hasn't happened yet.

Dad attended an Alzheimer's support group where, I believed, someone taught him how to care for a demented family member. For Dad, it meant more. It was a survival course and a chance to share war stories. Dad returned from those meetings more animated and with a lighter step. I should have recognized how much support my dad needed. It wasn't until Mom became our responsibility that I felt the true weight of his burden.

Dad called me on another day. This conversation didn't start with any greeting.

"I THINK *it's time for your mother to stop driving."*
*"Has anything happened? Did she have an accident? Get lost?"*
*"No."*
*"But you think it's time?"*
*"It's time."*
*"Ok," I said, confused by the brevity of our conversation.*
*"Why don't you come on over and talk to her about it. Tell her it's time."*

I BELIEVED it would be family intervention, but I was mistaken. Mom sat beside me, our thighs touching, while Dad sat across the room with the newspaper pulled up over his face. I understood my role, Dad expected me to break the news to her. I didn't know the answers to her questions— what she'd done wrong or why she could no longer drive— and there was no movement behind the newspaper.

Considering we were both confused about what triggered

the conversation, mom was surprisingly accepting of the decision. She announced she preferred looking out the window instead of driving. But the next day, she changed her mind. Dad did not escape the intervention. Every day afterward, he had to remind her about the decision. He hid the keys and eventually gave her car away.

～

I DROPPED my hours at work to spend more time with Mom. I imagined that we'd travel, take in museums, movies, and restaurants. In short, I wanted Mom to enjoy her last days doing things that I thought she *should* like. My approach was wrong.

At first, Dad shook his head when I showed up at the door. "We don't need anything," he'd say with a perplexed expression. "Why are you here?" I thought I'd made a mistake, but with time, dad would start his shuffle toward the back door as soon as he heard my key in the front door. Sometimes, I'd just see a backward wave as he made his way toward his car and freedom.

Each week I planned a different excursion for the two of us. Mom trailed behind me at the museum. I'd point out a piece of artwork, and she'd smile indifferently and nod her head without enthusiasm. Half-way through the gallery, I realized she wasn't interested, so we cut through a corridor and headed to the parking lot. She thanked me on the way home. More, I'm sure, just for the occasion of spending time together, than the experience of looking at paintings and bronze statues.

The next week I tried a visit to the arboretum, something she'd enjoyed in the past. How could admiring flowers and enjoying the sunshine possibly go wrong? We chatted about

23

the television show she'd seen the night before, the grand-children's activities, and her preference for a certain sunscreen. While she appeared content with the stroll, the cultivated landscape and its orderly rows of brightly hued blossoms failed to hold her interest. Determined to find something to make her smile, I pulled her into the restaurant overlooking the gardens.

I didn't count on the menu being confusing to her. Every drink and dish had to be explained and ultimately, she looked at me helplessly, unable to make a decision. I ordered her a tuna fish sandwich, passing over the seafood stuffed avocado and chicken piccata. For the first time, I recognized my mom's need for the familiar. This wasn't the time to explore new horizons, Mom craved simple and ordinary activities and routines.

She grinned when she took the first bite and I felt like I'd won a prize. Several glasses of ice tea later, we both needed to go to the bathroom. One of the two stalls was flooded with what I hoped was rainwater, but probably not. I maneu-vered her into the other stall and saw the problem. The toilet, with its industrial U shape, did not look like her own, and a shiny metal contraption on the wall hid the toilet paper. We navigated through these issues only to realize that she did not understand how the door latch operated. I held the door closed, listened as she pivoted in a circle, and then sighed when she finally plopped down on the seat. I was still grip-ping the top of the metal frame to hold it in place when my cell phone rang.

I hooked one foot under the door to keep it from swinging open and stood like a stork on the other leg when I took the call. I looked up information, answered questions for the caller, and then nearly lost my balance when Mom pulled at the door.

I finished my call and then took her place in the stall, dismayed to find that I could not see her through the narrow slits on the side of the doors. Worried that she would walk out of the bathroom and get lost, I hurried through my task and flung the door open. Mom was leaving the flooded stall, and liquid dripped from her fingers. Had she put her hands in the toilet? Touched the wet floor? The hygiene freak in me panicked. I rushed her to the sink and scrubbed her hands, dismayed by my failure to control the situation.

I'd run out of ideas, but Mom had her purse ready and a destination in mind on my next visit. "I want to go to Wal-Mart," she said. "I need to pick up a few things." Mom directed me to the parking spot and then motioned me toward the door nearest the carts. She had a routine there, knew most of the employees, and more then one of them stopped to chat with her as she made her way down the aisles. This was a bold and confident side of my mother that I'd never seen. She stopped to hug a burly man stocking frozen foods and then beamed like a child when we put the bags in the car. Wal-mart was mom's happy place, and we visited frequently in the coming years.

We also visited her gynecologist, where she decided to stop doing pap smears and mammograms. At her family doctor's office, she refused her next colonoscopy. But when she complained of vision problems, I made an appointment with her eye doctor.

Rain pelted the car windshield on the way to the appointment, but Mom was unconcerned. She had a way of trusting you with her personal safety that was both rewarding and humbling. While I worried about hydroplaning on the busy highway, Mom commented on the music playing on the radio. One of my favorite memories of Mom was when I was a teenager and Arethra Franklin's *Respect* came on the radio. I

smothered a giggle when she belted out the lyrics, but I looked at her differently after that day. Unassuming house-wife? *Yes*. Woman confident enough to acknowledge her own inner greatness. *Also, yes*.

We drove by a bakery known for its danishes, and I reminded her of the trips we'd made to a similar pastry shop after Sunday mass years earlier. My little sisters debated the virtues of fruit versus cinnamon swirl, but I always picked the cream cheese. We savored the memories and looked forward to a treat after the appointment.

Massive glass windows surrounded the waiting room of the ophthalmologist's office in the high-rise building down-town. Lightning slashed the sky, the thunder shook the glass, and the rain transformed the city below to an Impressionist's painting with grey and sombre tones. We each took one of the dog-eared magazines and sat down, waiting our turn.

When a young woman wearing shrubs and sneakers called her name, we followed her to another room, where she grilled Mom with difficult questions like: "Have you had any surgeries?", "Do you have any medical problems?", and "Are you taking any medications?". My mother deferred to me after announcing her name and date of birth. Despite being a standard line of questioning for a doctor's office, but I found myself irritable with the inter-rogation. Mom was sensitive about her diagnosis, even embarrassed by it, flinching at the word "Alzheimer's" in conversations. I gave vague answers since I'd already given her medical information to the office, and I relied on the staff consulting their own chart before the exam. Another mistake.

The medical assistant encouraged Mom to take a seat in the center of the examination room. It took Mom a few seconds to figure out how to climb into the chair, but this went unnoticed. The woman mumbled to herself as she

shone lights into my mother's eyes. "Why are you here again?" she asked.

"My mother says she's having trouble seeing," I answered.

Mom looked like a child, sitting obediently with her hands in her lap, listening to our conversation.

The woman made a wry face at the vagueness of the complaint, but continued. "Ok, let's get started. I'm going to show you the vision chart, and I want you to blink a lot when you read it."

Mom cocked her head at the assistant. "You want me to blink a lot?"

"Yes, blink a lot." she answered impatiently. Blinking lubricates the eyes. Blurred vision can be a consequence of dry eyes, so I knew the doctor's assistant wanted to ensure a good examination.

Mom nodded.

"Ok, read the first line."

With the same emphasis of a quarterback calling out signals to the center, Mom barked out the letters:

"E—D—F" followed by, and in compliance to the command, the word "BLINK".

The woman startled, swiveled on her stool to inspect the vision chart as if the word "blink" would show up on the third line. Mom continued.

"P—E—C—BLINK."

I held up my magazine so the assistant couldn't see my smirk. The assistant looked flustered now, but Mom was on a roll.

"F—O—D—BLINK."

Mom was 'blinking' a lot, and it didn't take long for the woman to get frustrated. She pulled the equipment away from Mom's face, jotted some quick notes, and looked annoyed as she exited the room.

She left Mom and I alone in a room with no windows. We

made small talk, listened to the thunder as the storm drew closer, and waited. The doctor had a Napoleonic presence and wore a pristine starched white coat. He started his exam —instructed my mother to look up, down, and to the side. He grew impatient when she did not immediately follow his commands and started snapping his fingers in the direction he wished her to look. Like a command to a pet dog.

It had been a mistake not to remind the office about her Alzheimer's. I wondered about finding a different provider for mom's care. Someone more tolerant of her condition. Perhaps one of the pediatric ophthalmologists would be willing to do her future examinations. The thunder crashed as I plotted our next steps, and then the lights flickered and went out.

Briefly, I considered whether God had struck the building in punishment for the doctor's cold attitude. Before I finished that fantasy, the doctor stood up, clicked on a small flashlight from his pocket and declared, "I can't work like this." He used the light to guide himself to the door and then walked into a hallway lit by adjacent windows. The door drifted shut behind him, plunging us into darkness.

I inched my way across the room, squeezed Mom's hand, and for long minutes we waited in the pitch-black. The doctor returned once the electricity was restored. He finished a brief exam, pulled back his chair and repeated his assistant's previous question. "Why are you here?"

His voice sounded accusatory, and I went on the defensive. "My mom says she is having trouble seeing," I repeated.

"There is nothing wrong with her eyes. She just needs reading glasses." He slammed the chart down on the side counter and huffed out of the room, acting insulted over the waste of his time. Mom bit her lip and looking guilty. I put my arm around her shoulder, finished up the billing paperwork, took her to the car.

We choked down cheese danishes at a small table still dotted with the crumbs and coffee rings of past customers. Neither of us spoke much. The storm's fury had died, but the rain still pelted the smudged window relentlessly. The world was murky, grey, and bleak. When the heat of the bakery became too stifling, I took her home.

*"Life is like a beautiful melody, only the lyrics are messed up."*
— Hans Christian Andersen

*A*s Mom's Alzheimer's progressed, we went through a variety of medications with the neurologist. On one occasion, my dad called for help with her prescribed patch. I discovered Mom had trouble retrieving the patch from the package, recognizing she needed to remove the plastic backing to reveal the sticky part, manipulating the patch, and placing it on correctly. Watching her handle it, or attempt to, made me realize that either dad would have to manage her medicines, or we'd have to make a change.

My sisters and I had serious discussions about assisted living centers, and I had rosy fantasies about the next stage of their lives. They could be served their meals in a dining room instead of Dad driving out for fast food several times a day. Dad could hang out with other men and "shoot the shit".

Rumors of shopping trips, holiday parties, even wine and cheese in the evenings sweetened the proposal. Dad's trips to the senior center declined, and I suspected the distance from the parking lot to the building was a factor. His limp steadily worsened, and he exhaled loudly when he reached his chosen destination. The pressure would be off Dad, and Mom would receive the extra help she needed.

It sounded perfect.

With his cane in hand, Dad plowed through the entry of the assisted living center and headed straight toward the sofa. Mom and I followed. A woman approached us and introduced herself. She offered to show us around the facility, but dad pointedly ignored her.

"Are you ready to look around?" I asked him tentatively, unsure what to make of the situation.

"I'm fine here, you go ahead." Dad tightened his jaw and stared at me with his *don't you dare* look.

Mom and I agreed about the loveliness of the center after our tour. Floral centerpieces decorated the dining room tables and the aroma of freshly baked cookies scented the halls. Soothing colors, no stairs to navigate, and a charming interior courtyard accessible from all the resident's rooms. I was delighted, even excited, by the idea of moving my parents closer to me in the hotel-like environment, but when we finished the tour, Mom didn't think it would work. My heart sank.

"I don't have one of those." She pointed to a wreath with sprays of baby's breath popping out between pastel peach and creamy white flowers—a decoration on one of the resident's doors.

I hooked my arm through hers. "I'll buy one," I said. Dad was not so easy. He refused to make eye contact when we returned to the sitting area, and I knew better than trying to

push him. We gathered information, and I followed my stone-faced father to the car.

It took me some time to realize that Dad had no intention of moving. He planned on staying in their house and visiting his wife at her new dwelling. I thought him selfish at the time, but he was the better informed of the two of us.

"Something could happen to you, Dad." I leaned forward on the sofa, insistent, pleading. "Something will happen and she won't be able to get help." Mom could no longer operate a phone, and his health was declining. I accompanied him to an assortment of specialists: a cardiologist for his arrhythmia and elevated blood pressure, a pain specialist for his back, a hematologist for his low platelets. He was on an endless circuit of doctors and therapists.

Dad leaned back in a recliner with lumpy cushions shaped by years of supporting the same body. He fiddled with the newspaper, folded it once and then one more time before placing it on the side table. "Why do you have to be like that...so pessimistic?" He gave me a hard look, and I knew the conversation was over.

A few months later, I was pulled from an examination room to take a phone call from my parent's neighbor. "Something's happened to your dad," she said.

"Is he okay?" I asked.

"I'd rather not talk about it. Can you come right away?"

I don't know about other doctors, but I have a mode I switch on in an emergency. Emotions get brutally shoved into some closet and the door violently slammed shut. I had a task. From the brief conversation, I realized my father was dead and I had to get to my mother.

I parked my car on the street, behind the assortment of emergency vehicles with their lights still flashing in an endless rotation, and rushed up the steps. When I opened the door, she headed in my direction with her face stark and her

eyes wide with fear and grief. Her summer nightgown only came to her knees and was thin from too many washes. Her bare feet almost unhinged me, every protective instinct within me roared to life at her waif-like appearance. I wrapped my arms around her and wished I could tuck her some place safe, away from the strangers walking through her house. She pulled back from my hug and tried to explain.

"He's…He's…He's…He's…" I'd never heard a person stutter so dramatically and the harder she tried, the worse the stutter became. I reassured her, wrapped her in a spare jacket, and tried to figure out what happened. The neighbor filled in some gaps—Mom arrived on their doorstep, incoherent and agitated, earlier that morning. They thought she'd had a fight with Dad, so they sat her down and made her a cup of tea.

It was some time before they figured out what she was trying to say—that something bad had happened to her husband. They followed her to the house and then called for help. The obvious question is whether he was alive when she went in search of help. I'm not sure I want to know.

～

I TOOK Mom to my house, and for the first couple of days she was asleep or crying. During the scant periods in between, she'd walk around the house with a dazed expression. If I'd been less distracted by my own grief, I would have questioned why she asked to have a "wine party". Mom sipped on an occasional glass of champagne to celebrate the New Year and had a rare glass of wine with a fancy dinner. Ignoring the fact that this was out of character, and wanting to fulfill my mom's every wish, I made arrangements. I called family, made an assortment of appetizers, and bought several bottles of wine.

My daughter was the first to realize Mom was getting drunk. Mom's appetite was poor, and she'd not been eating well for days. She ignored the cheese and crackers, the sliced fruits and meats, and instead zeroed in on that oblivion-inducing liquid. A short time later, she was smiling widely, tipping her glass in my direction in a sloppy salute, and then stumbling around the countertop toward the living room.

It's an odd feeling when you become responsible for the woman that raised you, the one that set your curfew and doled out punishments when you broke the rules. And it's painfully distressing when your own daughter has to remind you of your duties. I got over my shock at seeing Mom weave around the room and then insisted she take bites from a plate that my daughter prepared. At the end of the evening, I slipped her an ibuprofen, cajoled her into drinking a glass of water, and tucked her in bed.

The next day we started clearing out her house and making preparations to move her into the assisted living center.

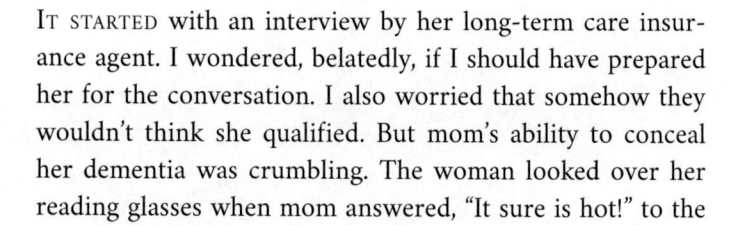

It started with an interview by her long-term care insurance agent. I wondered, belatedly, if I should have prepared her for the conversation. I also worried that somehow they wouldn't think she qualified. But mom's ability to conceal her dementia was crumbling. The woman looked over her reading glasses when mom answered, "It sure is hot!" to the question "What season is it?". She pressed her, "Would you say that it's fall, winter, spring or summer?"

Mom looked at me for help. I refused to meet her eye and instead looked out the window, pretending interest in the shrubbery outside. Mom finally answered, "I like all the seasons, don't you?" The woman waited a moment and then

continued with her evaluation. I turned my attention back to Mom when I saw her stand up.

The interviewer had asked her, "How do you take a shower?" and Mom took the question literally. She rushed to demonstrate how to turn the nozzle, pointed out her shampoo and then used a dry washcloth to mime the act of scrubbing her face. I'm not sure if this was a passing answer or not. The woman smiled benignly and then marked a box on a document that was several pages long.

Mom couldn't answer a majority of the questions, but the woman didn't pressure her like the neurologist had. In the end, mom looked pleased, as if this visitor was a long-lost friend and they'd enjoyed a pleasant afternoon catching up. They approved Mom's benefits.

AN ACQUAINTANCE GAVE a new mother advice: "You can't have a daycare that's too far away. When you drop your baby off, you're literally taking your heart out of your chest and leaving it behind. You won't survive if you're too far apart."

Mom and I picked out a decoration for her new door—red and white flowers with blue ribbons that curled and cascaded in a festive display. It exhibited a cheeriness that neither of us felt. A five-minute drive separated me from my mother, but I still wished there was some way to tuck her back into my chest where she belonged.

Mom had a lifetime of possessions to condense and our only purchases consisted of a shower curtain and a metal trash can. The apartment was a rectangular room with a dividing wall separating the area into two quarters. A full-sized refrigerator, a metal sink with a microwave attached above it, and a wall of cabinets was on the left side of the room. Against the opposite dividing wall, we placed a twin-

sized bed with a small bedside table. A statue of Mary with the glue yellowed from a previous repaired crack and a photograph of Dad, smiling confidently in a business suit, adorned her dresser.

We brought the blue and gold striped sofa from her living room because it was a sleeper sofa. A recliner and another dresser, which also served as a stand for the television, filled the second half of her room. It was an odd arrangement, but functional. The door leading to the outside courtyard was her favorite part of her new apartment.

When I left my daughter behind in a college dorm, I rationalized it was an important step toward her independence. I'm not sure what justification I was supposed to use when I left Mom behind. I walked alone toward my car, chased by guilt and doubt, on her first night alone in the assisted living. Mom met me at the entry early the next morning, before any of the other residents stirred from their beds. With her purse in one hand and her dog in the other, she charged toward my car as if escaping a burning building. In those first several weeks, she spent more time with her daughters, in our various houses, than she spent in her own new home.

Maya eased her transition more than any of us. She would insist on climbing up Mom's chest, peer into Mom's face with her chocolate colored eyes, and refuse to settle until she was satisfied that all was well. That diva dog distracted Mom better than any of us during those dismal months.

THE CAREFULLY MARKETED fantasy of these assisted living centers unraveled rapidly. The women residents formed high school like cliques, with invitations to tables extended to

certain residents. Seats were assigned by the grande dames, a fact lost on my mother, and newcomers had to earn a spot. When Mom invited her new friend to the table, a petite grey-haired spitfire with swollen joints in her hands and a bad back, she unknowingly created a problem. They refused to allow the woman to sit down and Mom got perplexed, then angry. They had to call in the director to handle the problem. Mom left her former table and started collecting the lost and bewildered, welcoming anyone to open seats, and pulling up chairs for late-comers.

Kitchen chefs arrived and departed faster than the seasons turned. On one day, her plate might feature a meal appetizing enough to grace the table of an expensive restaurant. The next day, a bologna sandwich on white bread with a side of bagged chips, prepared by the center's office staff when the cook abruptly quit. A partially filled plastic cup of inexpensive wine and a store-bought cookie defined happy hour. One resident snuck too much alcohol, and some undisclosed event transpired. It wasn't Mom—just in case you were wondering. They modified the activity calendar, replacing the Friday social hour with a game of bingo and a cup of cranberry juice. "Don't drink too much," an aide warned me. "That stuff is potent!" She wagged her finger in front of the pitcher to emphasize her advice before dashing away. I still don't know what would have happened if I drank a second glass.

I'd never considered the most distressing part of moving into an assisted living center. Thin walls separated the residents, and it wasn't uncommon to hear noises coming from your neighbor's apartment. Sometimes, the blare of a television compensated for a hearing-impairment. Or the sobs of a scared new resident, suffering the loss of a spouse, might wake you from your slumbers. On other nights, it was far worse.

The stretcher's squeaky wheels as it moved rapidly down a hallway, accompanied by the squawking of two-way radios and hissing of oxygen tanks. The play-by-play of the paramedics attempting a resuscitation. Mom looked shellshocked after those nights.

---

*To dance, put your hand on your heart and listen to the sound of your soul.*
— Eugene Louis (Luigi) Faccuito

om's Alzheimer's steadily worsened, creating more problems that needed solutions. The staff alerted me when she left the center to go on walks with other women. This brought up a host of concerns. Who were these women, and could I trust them to watch out for my mother? What if she wandered off, and they didn't notice? Her sense of direction had always poor, but now it was non-existent. What if she stepped off a curb into oncoming traffic? The center was located on a busy road with no sidewalks. It sounds like I'm talking about a child, right?

She was not a child, but she wasn't able to take care of herself any longer. I was tip-toeing on a razor's edge when I told my mother that I didn't think it was wise for her to walk with the ladies. Her gaze dropped to the floor, and I felt the

first bite of the blade. Mom threw herself against a nearby wall, flattened her hands on either side of her face, and then leaned her forehead against the surface. Her shoulders heaved.

"Mom?"

I didn't even know what I was asking. I'd been cut in half.

She pushed herself off the wall and faced me with tears coursing down her cheeks. "I've been a bad girl, haven't I? That's why I can't be with my friends anymore."

We'd just finished a conversation about a news story, and in the blink of an eye, she'd become a toddler, filled with remorse for an imagined broken rule. I wanted to reverse everything I'd said and allow her to do anything—everything—that she could possibly want to do. But at the same time, her response validated my concern. I needed to protect her.

I wrapped my arms around her and held her as she cried on my shoulder. My promises to take her on walks didn't make up for what I'd done. I punished my mother for the crime of succumbing to her illness and it made me sick inside.

~

THE ROOM KEY presented another issue. There's a fine line between wanting your privacy and getting locked out of your room. I figured we crossed it by the time I drove to Lowes and made the twenty-fourth copy of her key. I put each key on a neon-colored plastic bracelet that she could slip over her wrist when she left the room. The problem arose when she'd hide them in odd places: the microwave, her sock drawer, a random coffee cup, or tucked in with some dollars in a secret envelope in the top of her closet (in case she had an emergency). When I could, I would scour the room,

collect all the keys and put them in a basket. Within a few weeks, they'd disappear again.

Maya was a blessing and a spoiled prima donna who insisted on immediate gratification for every urge. It made sense to change her to dry food since it didn't require remembering how to open a can, but Maya's disdain made that impossible. We tried mixing wet food with dry, hoping to "wean" her onto the dry, but she'd meander up to the bowl, take a sniff and curl up her lip. She'd tire of a particular brand of canned food and go on hunger strikes till her ribs stuck out.

She started having accidents in the room. Perhaps "accidents" is the wrong word. I'm pretty convinced that those dark stains on the carpet were in retaliation for perceived insults. Any time we left Maya alone, we'd return to see a puddle or pile somewhere. Mom would standby helplessly as I scrubbed the floor. Her gaze bounced from me to the dog who'd climbed onto her bed and danced on her hind feet in anticipation of being picked up. "I don't know what to do. I can't spank her…" Her brows furrowed. "Can I?"

Mom needed more and more help. Reminders to rinse the shampoo from her hair, load the toothbrush with toothpaste, find the new roll of toilet paper tucked in a small cabinet in the bathroom. Oddly, she never forgot to put on lipstick and for a long time I thought her lips must be naturally rosy tinged. We had to update her care plan at the center to include more assistance with her routine tasks. The care plan is a checklist that the assisted living or memory care takes responsibility for. Charges are al la carte, like a menu, or each item is added to reach a final sum that falls into a pre-determined price range. As the need for care increases, the cost moves up.

Mom was mortified by the strangers who claimed they were going to help her with what she considered intimate

tasks. At her insistence, they stood outside her bathroom, calling out instructions as she went through her daily routine. "Put your bra on before the shirt!" or "Did you remember deodorant?" When a young man showed up on shower day, she crossed her arms over her chest and refused to budge until he left her room.

We hired an agency who promised a trio of rotating women, hoping for some continuity and more personal care. An expense no one counted on, but necessary. We were fortunate that Mom had a long-term care insurance, or this might not have been an option.

These new aides kept a log updating us on Mom's day-to-day life: *Judith had a fine morning. She drank two cups of coffee and enjoyed talking to her friends. We like to go outside in the courtyard.*

Patti was in her fifties, had curly grey-streaked hair and a scratchy voice that suggested a history of cigarette use. She let us know about Mom's incontinence.

"I don't like this...not one bit!" Mom waved the new disposable underwear in the air, but then lifted her leg so I could help her put the offensive item on.

I didn't know what to say to Mom, but Patti did. "I told her, we gotta keep your butt clean. Ain't no reason to be embarrassed." Patti figured out that mom's coffee intake had gone up dramatically and it was wrecking havoc on her intestines. She suggested switching her back to the tea she was used to. We purchased teabags and solved the problem. Patti tucked the bag of diapers on an upper shelf saying, "You'll be needing these later. No sense getting rid of them."

Delores had a capful of white hair, perfect posture, and a professional attitude. When she arrived to the room with her tote bag of necessities, it was clear she was on duty. An ex-nurse, she spoke in quiet and soothing tones that allowed no debate. She read the Bible out loud and wrote notes like:

*Judith only ate three-fourths of her lunch. She enjoyed the meat-loaf, but would not touch the green beans.* Was that disapproval I sensed in her comment? *Afterward she urinated and had a small bowel movement.*

Delores was a reincarnation of my grandmother who, I swear to God, found some way to return to earth to watch over my Mom. If you knew my grandma, this would not be shocking to you. She was bull-headed enough to force Jesus to make a small rip in the fabric separating us from the heavens, just big enough for her to slip through. Mom must've sensed it too. "This is Mother," she'd say when introducing her new aide. I'd grown up hearing Mom refer to her parents in the very formal titles of Mother and Father and when my uncle referred to my grandpa as "dad", it almost seemed disrespectful.

I'd hardly met the third aide before another woman replaced her. And then another.

My husband and I hired a series of nannies and babysitters when my children were young. When Tyranna started, my little boy mistakenly thought I'd said the new sitter's name was Tyrannosaurus, so he called her T-Rex. I hurried to correct him, worried she'd be offended by the comparison to a dinosaur. But when I discovered she was taking my children across town and giving them pocket change to buy treats while she spent hours in her hair salon, I fired her and started referring to her as T-Rex too. Heidi moved in with us next. She snuck out in the middle of the night and received mail with swastikas drawn on the envelopes. Sally was our Mary Poppins. It was the same with Mom and her aides, a series of matches and mistakes.

MOM HAD a melanoma removed from her nose years earlier,

but her new freckles were proof that while she remembered her lipstick, she no longer applied her sunscreen when she spent time in the courtyard. Landscaped with flowering shrubs, smooth river stones and a bubbling fountain, it was a common gathering place for the residents. They pulled together chairs and benches, gossiping about the newest cook or the absence of a particular woman at lunch, and the dog was allowed to sniff and pee.

Mom walked into this area in the middle of the night when her dog woke and barked by the door. Winter arrived with temperatures dropping to the thirties and she stepped outside without a coat and automatically locked the door behind her.

That same night, I awoke with an urgent sensation that Mom was in danger. I swiped my cell phone from the bedside table and checked the time. Slightly past two o'clock. I'd woken with a dry mouth and my heart hammering. In seconds, I had the center's number pulled up from my contact list. I stared at it, torn between calling and appeasing my fear, and feeling like a fool for reacting to what must've been a bad dream. I put the phone down, fluffed my pillow and reassured myself that my mother was surely asleep in her bed.

Each of the four sides of the courtyard had an unlocked clear glass door, larger than the resident's entrances, leading to sitting areas with comfy chairs and a generous sofa. Mom was not locked out, but she couldn't find her way inside either. A night shift worker, who happened to notice her jiggling a door knob of one of her neighbors, rescued her.

Mom shuddered when she told me the story the next morning. Maya, in her customary lounge in Mom's arms, perked up her ears up and sniffed the air around her as if trying to locate the cause of Mom's distress. "I was so scared," she said, "I thought I would freeze to death."

*Had God woken me from my sleep to deliver her from the freezing weather?* It was ridiculous to even entertain the notion; I was a person of science, not prone to flights of fancy. But then I read this: "The intuitive mind is a sacred gift, and the rational mind is a faithful servant. We have created a society that honors the servant and has forgotten the gift'. Words from a true scientist—Albert Einstein. Maybe I'd ignored my intuition.

*Rock Me Amadeus*
— Falco

*L*ike every other day, I knocked a few times to announce my arrival and then walked in to Mom's apartment. Patti met me at the door, and Mom appeared to be using her aide as a human shield. She peeked around Patti's neck and watched me with a worried expression.

"I've been meaning to talk to you about something..." Patti started.

I had to remind myself to breathe.

River stones from the courtyard covered every single horizontal surface in my mother's room—the top of the refrigerator, the small kitchen countertop, the dresser by her bed. They formed a single line across the top of the television. Rows of stones surrounded her bathroom sink and covered the toilet tank. Soft grays, speckled whites, salmon-

tinged tans, some with striations or dimples, all polished into muted matte tones that varied from the size of an apple to a large grapefruit.

"Mom?" My mind spun, and I felt like I'd walked through the door to some alternate universe or artist's installation.

"Your mom's been doing some rock collecting," Patti informed me. The corner of her mouth turned up into a half-smile, but I was too shocked to see the humor.

"I can see that," I said, careful to keep my tone neutral. Mom was biting her lip as she watched for my response, and I didn't want her to sense my alarm at the odd sight.

"We're trying to pick out our favorites and return the rest," Patti continued.

"I can help with that," I answered. I longed to return the room to order as fast as possible, to erase the evidence of her deranged thinking and fortunately, Mom was agreeable to our task. We each took armfuls of the stones and dumped them back into the courtyard, filling back in what had become markedly thinner spaces in the landscape. I pretended to ignore the times that mom spotted a new rock, one that shimmered when it caught the sunlight. Or another one that had a perfect egg shape. She'd tuck it under her shirt when she thought no one was watching and then find a hiding spot inside her small apartment.

For days afterward, I would continue to find those stones. In a drawer, tucked between her pajamas, inserted in the toe of a sneaker, behind her sofa, and even in the refrigerator. It was an Easter egg hunt each time I visited. With time she lost her fascination with the smooth stones. I have to say though, I'd never looked closely at those rocks before. You know what? They're quite pretty.

∾

IT TOOK me five hours to figure it out. Despite my routine care of tiny humans, not yet capable of language, I failed my mother. I arrived to find her curled up in her bed and the staff informed me she'd been vomiting. I have no memory of my mother being sick during my childhood, but countless recollections of her putting cool washcloths on feverish foreheads and rubbing the upset tummies of her daughters. This changed when she started the medicines to slow the progress of her Alzheimer's. At first we thought she had a stomach bug. And then another. The episodes came faster and faster until I realized her abdominal pain and vomiting were a reaction to her medicines. She'd return to normal when we stopped a drug, and it would take months of the new drug before the same side effects would appear.

On that day, I blamed her medications again, but didn't rule out the possibility it could be a viral infection. I took her temperature and pushed her to sip an electrolyte enhanced sports drink. Her eyes were closed, her face was chalky white, and she moaned with discomfort. It was only when she drew her fingers to her temple and winced that I made the connection. "Do you have a headache?"

Her eyes flew open. "Yes!"

After few ibuprofen and a brief nap, she was a new woman. Her first migraine taught me she could no longer alert anyone when she was hungry, sick or in pain.

More confusing medical issues followed. When a visiting physician, checking up on mom's cold symptoms, asked if she had chest pains, she answered "yes". Her cardiac work up at the emergency room was normal.

An urgent trip to the family dentist when she informed me she'd lost a tooth. She hadn't.

And then the *spells* started. Randomly, her eyes would shutter closed, and her body would sway precariously. Just as you'd reach out your arms to catch her in what appeared to

be an imminent faint, her eyes would pop open again. It was weird. We called them "sinking spells" as if a good tonic would fix the situation.

~

MOM'S CLOTHING WAS SHRINKING. When we complained, they blamed mother's weight gain for the problem. She was less active and eating more, but she wasn't getting taller. There had to be a reason her pale ankles peeked out from under the hem of her pants. It proved easier to buy new clothes than introduce a change in the laundry department who washed and dried all of her clothing on the hot setting.

On one shopping day, Mom applied her pink lipstick and rummaged through her drawers for her handbag (which she still hid despite having no money in her wallet). Along with her keys, her purses disappeared with regularity, so we added another item to our shopping list. Her favorite purchase, despite being designed for tweens wearing mismatched socks and unicorns on their tee-shirts, had been a purple clutch with sparkly lavender stars. When it disappeared, I tore up her room searching for it to no avail. We stopped by her mailbox on the way to the car and Mom pointed toward a side corridor. "That's the dungeon," she said casually, still picking through the various envelopes and grocery store ads. I glanced in the direction she'd pointed. The locked memory care unit resided at the end of the hallway. "Look at this! I've got coupons!" she exclaimed.

~

I CARRIED an armful of pants and blouses to the changing room and waited outside for my mother to show herself. The first pair of pants was too loose around her waist, so I

encouraged her to try on the next pair. A few minutes later she emerged wearing the same outfit. I peeked under the door, saw the pants fall to the ground, and then backed away so she wouldn't realize that I spied on her. The third time she presented herself, she had the same outfit on.

In concession to her intense modesty, I darted into her dressing area and averted my eyes while she instinctively covered her torso with a random shirt. I tucked the pants and its matching shirt under my arms, shoved a new outfit into her startled arms, and bolted out again. When she needed new bras, I fastened them with my eyes closed and then peeked to examine the fit when I thought she wasn't looking.

I searched for easy clothing. A sheer blouse, with the cami attached inside, was a nightmare to put on. Long sleeved tee-shirts over elastic waisted pants became the new uniform. We added a cardigan or zippered sweat shirts in cooler weather. Slip-ons replaced tennis shoes.

Mom had never been interested in shopping for clothing, and she still wore outfits I remembered from my childhood. But when her weight increased and her clothing shrank, it became necessary to eliminate mom's once eternal wardrobe. She enjoyed admiring herself in her new outfits, trendy tops with splashy colors and sequins, but my throat grew uncomfortably thick when I gathered up her old clothes. I caressed the sweaters, rubbed my fingers across the cotton shirts, folded them into rectangular piles...all while a stream of memories played in an endless loop in my head. When I dropped them off at the donation center, I felt like I left pieces of my mother behind.

*Where words fail, music speaks.*
—Hans Christian Andersen

*I* wish someone had warned me how distressing it is to visit a memory care for the first time. Mom steadily worsened during her three years in the assisted living center, and we needed to identify her next dwelling. The investigation of these facilities invariably left me seeking the safety of my own home and a strong drink.

The first one looked clean and bright, but smelled of unwashed bodies and urine. I forced myself to continue the tour. Placement of the residents into each "neighborhood" was based on the severity of their illness. I persevered through three of the four neighborhoods, smiled wanly at my tour guide, and insisted I'd seen enough. I saw my mother in the faces of those residents, watched her decline before my eyes, and I wasn't prepared to witness the end-stage in the last neighborhood.

Worried that Mom would not be able to identify her room, I asked if we could place something familiar outside her doorway. The woman shrugged her shoulders, "It might not be such a good idea. Do you see those?" She pointed toward a few plastic plants at the end of the hallway. "We call those pee-pots. The more confused men will urinate on them. They'd probably do the same thing...." I swallowed hard. After the tour ended, I almost sprinted to my car.

Trees lined the streets on my way to option two, a home tucked into a community setting. Someone swept the walkway clean of debris, and from the outside, the ranch house could have been mistaken for someone's home. The knots in my stomach, still present from my last tour, unraveled.

The dreary living room had a multitude of recliners filled with residents who stared with glazed eyes at a movie playing on the television. Their mouths gaped listlessly. In contrast, the owner was chirpy and full of energy. "Tell me what your mother likes to eat," she insisted. "I like to stock the food my people like!" She discussed her strategies for bathing resistant individuals and showed me the alarms that prevented residents from wandering outside the confines of the house in the middle of the night. When I closed the door behind me, I blinked at the brightness of the sun.

Too mentally exhausted to explore further, we chose the memory care associated with the assisted living center she was already in. They, too, had rows of recliners with residents in various stages of decline. But at least they had light. And an odd stuffed toy seal that would arch its tail and make purring noises in response to stroking its back. "That's weird," Mom said, when she saw it. I agreed. Choosing a memory care, however, is not the same as moving in.

~

"LIE TO HER?" I'd run into a friend of mine at a fundraiser, and she was relaying her own mom's advice. I didn't understand.

"She told me that as she gets older, the best thing to do was to just *lie* to her." We stopped talking, and the music swelled in our silence. I nodded, but couldn't imagine a situation where I'd lie to my mother.

There was some mild disagreement on the right time to move Mom into the memory unit. No one doubted her ultimate destination, but deciding to move someone into a dungeon, as she still referred to it, was an emotionally charged discussion.

One sister made the arrangements to move her furniture, while another took her out for the day. My sister called me later that afternoon.

"What do I say? What do I tell her when I have to take her down a different hallway," her voiced dropped, "to a different room?"

My friend's words came back to me and I told her, "Lie to her".

My sister didn't understand. "What do you mean?"

"Tell her that something went wrong with her room. A water leak, electric problem…make up something. Tell her she has a *new* room."

My sister was dubious, but it worked. In a matter of a few hours and very little fanfare, Mom and Maya were locked into the memory unit. Her new quarters surrounded a small courtyard, a mimic to her previous quarters. The colors and decor were similar too. Possibly the familiarity helped Mom's transition. For whatever reason, moving Mother into a locked ward was disturbingly easy.

*A SLIGHT PAUSE HERE. Allow me to orient you. Visiting a memory care is like an unexpected trip to another country where they don't always speak English. The customs and routines differ from what you're used to. The apparel, or lack thereof, may be shocking. While your tour guides do their best to remain pleasant and helpful, the natives are under no such obligation.*

*I'm a frequent flier, moving between the two countries on a regular basis. My passport is nearly full, and I've adapted to the contrast between what I used to consider a normal life versus the ever-changing terrain of the Alzheimer unit.*

*What follows are more glimpses of my visits to this foreign land. Some excerpts are choppy, with no apparent conclusion. I, too, wish I knew how the story ended. The turnover rate of both the tour guides and the natives is high, the former because the job is difficult. The later needs no explanation.*

*It's a disconcerting and bewildering experience. Do your best to hang in there. My mom used to say that. It's good advice in just about any situation.*

~

*MOM ATTACKED AN AIDE.* I read the message on my phone twice, not able to conceive of any situation where the words could be true. It was.

Mom's toilet was not flushing, and although I'd reported the situation, nothing happened. The toilet was full of waste, and the bathroom smelled bad. I suspect Mom refused to use the toilet until it became urgent and this situation caused her first urinary tract infection. The doctor ordered ABH gel when the staff contacted him about her aggression. Mom looked suspicious as the aide rubbed the clear medicine on her bare arm.

ABH gel is a combination of Ativan, Benadryl and Haldol. Ativan is used for anxiety, Benadryl is an allergy medicine

with a side effect of drowsiness, and Haldol is a medication prescribed for psychosis. The last drug disturbed me. An aide tried to reassure me, telling me the medicine was not "getting inside" her, but I knew better. The fire left Mom's eyes, and she became drowsy and limp. When they started an antibiotic for her urinary tract infection, her demeanor return to normal. Later on, we discovered a multitude of reasons for behavior changes; bladder infections always topped the worst offender list.

We spent hours in the courtyard in her new abode, and Maya was our source of entertainment. Together we watched her examine a line of ants traveling across the pavement, pee on a nearby shrub, or snore in Mom's lap. I learned to be careful with our conversations and asked only questions that I was confident she could answer. Inquiring what she had for breakfast, for instance, might bring a distressed look to her face. "Are you cold?" or "Are you hungry" required no recall of an event that occurred hours earlier. She remained interested in her grandchildren's activities and liked the donuts I brought. Life settled into a new normal.

$\approx$

WHEN MY DAUGHTER learned to drive, the online program recommended against telling your novice student to *stop* as this would cause them to brake too abruptly. Instead, they urged, say "slow to stop", which in my case came out…"Slow-to-stop…Slow-to-stop…Slow-to-stop."

It was this phrase that popped in my head when I turned the corner of the memory center and saw my mother running toward me. She was pink-cheeked, out of breath, and pushing a stranger's wheelchair as she ran. The woman, with bleached blue eyes and thinning hair pulled into a feeble

ponytail, was wide-eyed and hyperventilating. Her fingers blanched in their desperate grip on the armrests. Mom came to a dramatic stop in front of me.

"Whatcha doing?" My gaze flitted across the living area and down the hallways. Various residents, some in chairs and others making slow progress with their walkers, populated the hallways, but not a single aide was in sight.

"Exercising. I'm going round and round," answered Mom with a grin. She released her grip on the push handles and waved in a demonstration of her circuit. When her captive sensed Mom's release on the handle, she leaned forward, planted a slippered foot on the ground and strained in a puny attempt at a get-away. Mom saw the slight movement and her hand snaked out to regain her grip on the wheelchair. The woman dug her heels in the carpet, and gritting her teeth, pulled with all the might her frail body was capable of.

"I'm helping her exercise, too," Mom explained.

The hapless victim stared at me with eyes that implored me to intervene.

"Let's find Maya. I bet it's time to take her outside," I told my mom. "You've had enough exercise for now."

---

*Catch Me Now I'm Falling*
— The Kinks

*M*om was outraged. I found her stomping down the hallway, full of complaints and accusations. "They made me work all night long!" she spat out. "I didn't sleep at all!" Purple circles traced her lower lids, and her face was drawn and pale. When I took her hand in mine, planning to sweet talk her into a nap, she winced. "He hurt me!" she claimed, pointing to a swollen joint on her finger.

She might have tripped over her dog. Might've slipped and flung out her hand to catch herself. I figured it would be impossible to discover how she'd been injured, but when I pushed up her sleeves, I found more bruises in the shape of fingers gripping her forearms. When I stopped an aide and asked about the injuries, she shrugged her shoulders and advised talking to the director. Mom stared at the discolored smudges and shuddered until I pulled down her sleeves. I

walked Mom to her room for a nap, and then knocked on the director's door.

"Could it have been one of the men?" I asked. Diced carrots, noodles and pieces of beef flew everywhere when a new resident threw his plate across the dining area. Another resident stomped a circular route that brought him to the locked exit. He grabbed the doorknob, wrenched and rattled the door until a staff member redirected him. Then he resumed his course.

The director wouldn't meet my eyes. "The male attendants are not allowed near your mom," she answered. The breath stilled in my throat at her words. I hadn't even considered *the staff workers*. My head was still spinning on how difficult it must be for the staff to protect residents from each other.

When my sister checked on her later, she found Mom walking the halls with a butter knife in her clenched fist. With each squeak of a wheelchair or the unexpected appearance of an aide, she raised her weapon with a yelp. My sister packed a few days worth of clothing and toiletries and took her home.

Have you seen those books where children use water on a paintbrush to unveil the colors of the picture? Purple blotches appeared on Mom's arms, shoulders, and back when my sister helped her with her shower. She photographed the injuries and sent us nauseating images of her battered skin. I thought about those marks on mom's body later that night. I imagined the retribution I wanted to demand for the harsh handling of a feeble, demented woman. My oath to "do no harm" and my Christian duty to "turn the other cheek" would prevent me from actually hurting someone. I think.

Reporting abuse appears meaningless. Mom pointed to one particular attendant, but she was not capable of describing the incident, and bruises aren't enough evidence.

For months afterward, the sound of a deep voice would cause her to tremble and dart for cover—in a room, around a column or behind my back.

We moved her to another facility and learned that we weren't the only ones who'd jumped ship. Each time a resident disappeared from the memory care, I assumed they'd died. Previous neighbors, back from the grave, greeted us when we arrived and they shared their own stories for transferring facilities. I'm ashamed to say that we should've formed a support network from the beginning. Kept track of each other and sent out warnings of what we'd observed. But it just seemed too much. My life already had enough drama, and I craved shopping trips with girlfriends and movie dates with my husband, not swapping war stories with another worn-out caretaker.

Naive aides made the situation worse when they tried to desensitize Mom by taking her into stranger's rooms or encouraging conversations with the male residents. Bleary-eyed from poor sleep, she wavered between anxious vigilance and arm-flinging hostility. Fear became her baseline emotional state. "She's afraid of all men and I don't think you can change that," I told an aides when I discovered her goal. We notified the doctor, and he prescribed a medicine for anxiety.

~

MOM'S *SPELLS* WORSENED. She still insisted on attending mass weekly—she'd run a comb through her hair, put on some lipstick, and sling a purse over her shoulder. We'd emptied her handbag of anything of importance, leaving behind some photos, tissues and a few dollars for church. I only forgot to slip the money inside her purse once. When the offering basket came down the pew, her fingers clawed at the inside

of her bag. Her frantic expression transformed to resignation when her search failed to yield the desired paper, whose value she no longer understood. Dollar bills from my wallet, offered to her when I realized my oversight, didn't fulfill her sense of duty, and she looked morose for the remainder of the service. Her wallet was never empty after that day.

I'd like to believe that if Jesus was giving a church service, he'd pause when mom passed out right in the middle of "Amazing Grace". The priest didn't. There was no interruption of mass when she fell to the ground unconscious. By the time the paramedics arrived, her dazed eyes blinked opened. I wracked my brain trying to figure out what caused her spells. A brain tumor? Heart arrhythmia? And how aggressively would we treat whatever it was?

The diagnosis and treatment turned out to be simple. Mom tumbled out of her dining room chair after a particularly bad spell, and they called the paramedics. She nodded at us as we arrived at the emergency department, but otherwise slept through her entire evaluation: the cold stethoscope on her chest, the hands palpating her belly, the transfer to a gurney to wheel her to radiology for a CT scan. She even slept through the needle piercing her skin to get blood work. We obtained a list of Mom's medications from the memory care and I realized, for the first time, that her doctor had placed her on additional medications for anxiety—without informing us.

I understood his intention. Mom was a wreck after the assault, and the staff had to deal with her alternating fear and rage. He gave her an oral antipsychotic medicine which was, he claimed when we talked to him afterward, commonly used in dementia patients. He didn't take into account her sensitivity to medications, and this one caused sedation. Mom slept through the first two days of her hospitalization during which time she was extensively evaluated by a cardi-

ologist, internist, and a neurologist. She was prodded, scanned, and examined till they had nothing left to offer. They discharged her when she finally woke up.

I am perplexed by doctors who visit memory centers and make decisions without consulting or informing the family. As a pediatrician, it's as if I assign the daycare the responsibility of administering medications to a child without discussing it with a parent first. It's infuriatingly common. We switched doctors and the next physician was willing to consult the family and continue the wean from the antipsychotic medicine. Her spells diminished, and we learned to associate her wobbly days with prior sleepless nights. The spells weren't the only problem the medications caused.

～

MOM ENJOYED GOING FOR WALKS. Whether it was the sunshine, the breeze that ruffled her hair, or the antics of the dogs—a stroll lifted her spirits. Her interpretations of once common events made me smile. On one occasion, the utility company spread markers over our street's front lawns. "That's very nice," she said, nodding in approval. "What are we celebrating?"

Maya, her chihuahua, was a dainty walker with a stubborn streak. My dog, Tex, was a rambunctious, impulsive dork. He'd stop, dart, lunge, and invariably get tangled in Maya's leash. She laughed at his goofiness. Perhaps his foolishness distracted her, and that's how she missed seeing the shift in the sidewalk. In slow motion, I saw her stumble. I grabbed for her upper arm, slowing but not preventing her collision with the concrete. Her white-face, bewildered expression contorted to one of pain, and I was sure she'd broken her hip. We arranged for an X-ray.

I was celebrating that it was her wrist, not her hip, that

was fractured and almost missed what the orthopedic doctor said. "Surgery?" I repeated, stunned by his announcement. He explained her bones would continue to shift out of alignment and produce chronic pain if he didn't repair the injury. We admitted her to the hospital.

Despite her diagnosis on every form and chart, I still found that hospital staff would address Mom when they asked their questions. With sometimes bitter amusement, I would watch to see how long it took before they figured out that her answers might not be sufficient to their cause.

Nurse: "Are you allergic to anything?"

Mom: "1940"

Nurse: "I asked if you were allergic to anything" (said a little louder)

Mom: "What is this?" (pointing to her hospital gown)

Nurse: "To any medicines...Are you allergic to any medicines?"

Mom: "Maybe later we can have some lunch." She directed her comment to my sister, but then smiled at the nurse. "You can come too."

When Mom woke, she asked about her daughters and grandchildren by name. She was more lucid than I'd seen for months and my mind whirled...was it the anesthesia? A restful sleep? Coincidence? Ultimately, just another oddity of her illness.

The surgeon gave his report and explained that her bones were fragile. "It was like drilling through butter," he said. "She needs to wear a splint and keep the arm stationary." I work with children. Splints only stay on if children want them to stay on. I reminded him of her condition, but he encouraged me to "give it a try". We took her back to the memory unit, instructed the staff on her post-op care, and hoped for the best.

They forgot to give her the pain medication.

Sometime in the night, she removed the splint and put it in a magazine rack next to an outdated calendar featuring different puppies for each month. Like a wounded animal, her shiny eyes darted around the room feverishly. She paced the length of the room, cradling the injured wrist in her opposite hand. I called the surgeon.

Mom picked out a pretty spring green color for the cast. She was calm, and even interested, as they wrapped first the padding, and then casting material, around her forearm. The next morning I found the cast on her bed. She shook with rage and pointed at it. "I…don't…like…that!" Her wrist was swollen, and I worried that she'd damaged or possibly infected the surgical site. The orthopedic doctor reassured me, and then ordered a long arm cast that she could not wiggle out of.

The next day, I found pieces of the padding scattered all over her room and random white fibers clinging to her sweater. She sat in an armchair and smiled when she recognized me. The sight of the cast and the shredded padding proved too much for me. I fell to my knees in front of her and closed my eyes at the hopelessness of it all.

She patted me on the head like I was a little girl. "You worry too much," she said. "You've got to learn to let some things go." Her eyes met mine. Moments like this add to the surreal nature of the disorder. Did she understand what she'd done? I shook my head, helped her to her feet, and used moleskin to cover the rough edges of the cast.

Mom and I walked the courtyard a short time after her cast was removed. I'd anchored her arm with mine, but her foot slipped anyway. I could hear the surgeon's voice saying "bones like butter" as she crumpled to the ground. Staff ran toward us from all directions. I searched her face for any signs of distress, but this time she swiped the mulch from her pants and stood up.

Her clumsiness and teetering walk, that I attributed to her age or Alzheimer's, improved as we weaned her medications. And something else changed, too. Her body started responding to familiar tunes with a roll of a shoulder or a skip in her step. She started dancing.

I'd only seen mom dance once before her Alzheimer's diagnosis. On that evening, she pulled off her rubber gloves when she finished washing the dishes. The she took a seat in her customary recliner to read the newspaper. Rod Stewart's album, *It Had to be You: The Great American Songbook,* had just been released and was getting a lot of radio time. It had compilations of the classic crooner songs like "You Go To My Head" and "I'll Be Seeing You".

When Rod's raspy voice purred "The Very Thought of You", Dad popped out of his chair and held out his hand. Mom shook her head and continued her study of the grocery ads. She gave a mock gasp when he pulled her onto her feet.

Dad was a coarse man. He drank more than he should, cursed when he felt it was appropriate, and retreated into a shop in the garage to hit things with a hammer when life overwhelmed him.

His meaty hand clasped hers delicately, loosely, as if he held a small bird in his hand instead of the wife he'd had for four decades. They were an unlikely, graceful pair of dancers and he led her around the living room with no stumbling or missteps. He waggled his brows at me and commented on how good they'd been "back in the day". She twirled underneath his raised hand, a dainty extension of his own arm. I was mesmerized.

10

*Music touches us emotionally, where words alone can't.*
— Johnny Depp

He looked like an aging movie star when I saw him working in the courtyard. Grey hair angled rakishly over a square face, lean frame, and pants low on his narrow hips. He wore a long sleeve plaid shirt despite the warmer weather and he was bent at the waist with his legs spread wide, working the dirt with a small shovel. One at a time he loosened the roots of a plant and then, having unearthed it, he'd flip it over his shoulder.

After repeating this several times, he stood up, stretched his back and then used his sleeve to wipe the perspiration from his face. His grin was broad, a Cheshire cat smile, when he looked at the pile of plants at his feet. I suspected the Farmer had been working all morning. It must've taken hours to pull up those newly planted pansies. I smiled at his pride and then took a seat next to Mom.

SUSAN BADARACCO

"Red, white and blue." The man approaching our table had smudged glasses and a booming voice. He nodded at the man wearing a blue polo shirt and asked him, "Are you inspired?"

I thought the blue shirt man was asleep, but his eyes flashed open and he blinked several times to orient himself. "What?" he asks.

The woman sitting beside Mom made the connection. She pointed to her own shirt (red) and then the polo shirt (blue) and finally the newcomer (white). "It's patriotic!" she announced.

"What?" Mister Blue shirt remained uncertain about the topic.

An aide dropped off a small salad in front of each resident. Iceberg lettuce, slices of tomato, shredded cheese and black olives. She wore pressed maroon scrubs and not a single hair dared escape her elastic hair tie. When Mom picked up pieces of olive with her fork and announced, "I don't like this," the aide answered firmly, "That is your salad".

The red-shirt woman must be on an unusual dietary restriction. Ranch dressed topped her serving of shredded cheddar cheese. When she tried scooping it up with her fork, some dressing splashed on her shirt, making her two-thirds of the red, white and blue. With the precision of a surgeon, mom used her fork to turn over each pale green leaf and uncover any tiny remnant of olives. She was so consumed with avoiding them, she forgot to eat. I borrowed her fork, put a piece of tomato on the tines, and moved it toward her mouth.

The woman beside us had eyes that crinkled like Mrs. Claus. She held a dinner roll close to my face and I didn't know what to say. Was she asking what it was? Wanting me to take a bite? I took a chance with, "It's your roll, it's good for you". I often say "it's good for you" to my mom and I'm

not even sure why. Maybe she said the same to me when I was little?

The woman pointed out an insignificant piece of dark crust on the bread. "Is it a bug?"

Her question shocked me. She must've trusted me because she took a bite when I reassured her. My mom can't remember her reading glasses any more. Her distance vision is fine, but she has trouble seeing things close up. (I know this because the eye doctor was so kind to point it out.) Does she see bugs in her food, too?

The woman behind me could no longer communicate. Her meal consisted of different colored pureed foods, and she used her knife to tap on her plate. Tap. Tap. Tap. I was contemplating why she had a knife when I realized her table mates began mimicking her actions. Tap. Tap. Tap.

More residents from other tables joined in, and the noise escalated to a deafening level. It was like being in the middle of an uprising and my insides tightened in response, but the various staff members looked indifferent. A woman filling up water glasses casually touched the instigator's hand as she walked by. The noisemaker released the knife and then grabbed a fistful of the mashed food and brought it to her mouth. Crisis averted.

∼

WHILE I CLOSED my eyes and let the first warm rays of the spring sun warm my face, Mom launched herself out of her chair. She moved quickly, almost at a run, toward the center of the outdoor courtyard. I held my breath when she tripped on the edge of the sidewalk; memories of her broken arm were still too fresh. She caught herself, smiled mischievously, and opened her arms out wide.

"Father, do you see me?" she asked the clouds.

She wasn't talking to God. Grandpa worked for an airline, and she associated every overhead plane with his presence. The sound of an engine would cause her to look upward, point and smile. This time, it wasn't even a plane. I watched the bird, probably a hawk, as it swooped and plunged in mid-air. She was content, even happy, while she watched the same thing. Who was I to correct her? It didn't matter if it was a bird or a plane, anything that made her happy was okay with me.

Later, I gave her a hug and told her I was returning home. Her eyes moistened. "But I can't see you there." *That hurt.*

"I know, but I always come back. I will *always* come back." I said the same litany each time I departed, hoping, somehow, that it would help.

My mom shuttered her face and blinked the tears away. "You have to go now. It's time for you to go." In a blink, she'd transformed back into the woman who insisted that she not impose on any of her "girls".

*That hurt a lot.*

〜

THAT WEEKEND my adult children came home. In one glorious moment, I had my daughter on one side and my son on the other, and we were laughing and laughing over some insignificant joke. My heart almost burst with happiness. I am so proud of who they've become, but I miss them terribly. When Mom claimed my sister's move to another state was a crime against nature, I used to tease her. I get it now.

I got a lump in my throat waving to my daughter as she climbed into her car and felt teary-eyed saying goodbye to my son at the airport. Driving home, I wondered if Mom experienced this same elation and loss *every single time I visit her.*

*Knockin' on Heaven's Door*
— Bob Dylan

chalked it up to an odd day. When I arrived, the music selection had changed. Instead of Frank Sinatra and Dean Martin playing overhead, a female soprano's hymn filled the air. Aching and melodic, her voice rose as if filling the rafters of an ancient cathedral.

Mom stood up when she noticed me, and as usual, I tried to gauge her mood. Was she happy to see me? Would she recognize me? Mad or frightened by some real or imagined event? Somber eyes and a grim face met me. She pulled me aside from the other residents to have a private conversation. She spoke fervently, mostly nonsensical phrases, but with some disquieting words scattered in the prattle.

"Going away...rows of angels...be okay...God...with you again..." I chided myself for reading too much into her gibberish. The church service she'd attended earlier must've

impacted her somehow. Her eyes were filled with regret, and she touched my face gently as she spoke. I was unnerved by a conversation implying her imminent death.

When we encountered any of the employees, a man mopping the floor, a harried-looking woman pushing a cart of supplies, Mom would stop them and pay them compliments. "You're so beautiful" or "You work so hard". Mom was purposefully seeking her helpers, praising them and saying goodby—with a lot of confusing script in between. Or it was my imagination running wild?

I said goodbye when they slid her lunch plate in front of her. She gripped the armrests and rose as if to follow me. I kissed her on the cheek and pressed her shoulder down. "Eat your lunch," I insisted. "I'll see you again soon." It had taken a good five minutes to get her in the chair. She'd circled it, dragged it to the side and pushed it in without remembering to sit down.

Her eyes grew weepy and her sentences longer. "Never know the last time together" and "You will be okay". I tried to ignore her words, and instead, loaded her fork and directed it toward her mouth.

Another resident at the end of the table piped up, "What the hell is in this salad, anyway?" My mind listed the same ingredients I'd seen since Mom first arrived: iceberg lettuce, shredded cheddar, tomatoes and too much ranch dressing.

"The salad's not important," Mom scoffed. "We're together. I get to be with you for a while." It was the most rational sentence I'd heard in a long time.

A few days earlier my sister called, rattled by Mom's appearance after one of her spells. I tried analyzing the whole situation—the music, my sister's phone call, the sermon's effect on my mom, and ultimately I concluded it was an odd day.

But on the way home, I remembered reading in Mom's

journal about her waning appetite and ongoing complaints of abdominal pain. I thought of my grandmother, who'd had similar symptoms and then died in her sleep before the doctor determined the cause. The hole in my chest expanded as I drove.

~

AT FOUR O'CLOCK THE following morning, I clicked the app to the camera that allowed me to watch my mom. I zoomed in, peering at a fuzzy image of Mom's chest until I could make out the minute movements of the sheets that demonstrated she was breathing. For several seconds, my cell phone was was the only illumination in my bedroom. I finally clicked it off and stumbled to the kitchen to make myself a cup of tea.

~

THE FARMER'S A FLIRT. I've seen him holding hands and walking down the hallway with at least two different women now. The first was a stooped-over, white-haired resident in polyester pants. The second was a Hispanic woman with salt and pepper hair who alternated between shuffling and lurching like she'd had one too many drinks for lunch. Margarita didn't speak, but she smiled a lot, and if she was especially pleased by something you said or did, she'd clap her hands.

It wasn't uncommon to find him sitting beside his latest sweetheart, enjoying the afternoon in the shade of the porch. He'd pull out their chairs at lunch, assist these ladies to their feet, and offer spontaneous shoulder rubs. Always with a generous smile.

~

WHEN I ARRIVED AT LUNCH, Mom was holding a fork in one hand and the spoon in the other. I was unsuccessful in guiding either into her salad. The man to my right was a new resident; his shirt was buttoned incorrectly, causing the collar to rub against his unshaven chin. He held out his hands and commented, "I've been working around the house, look how filthy my nails are." He was right about his nails.

Most of his comments were directed at Mom. She answered him, "You can circle around and then put it on top, if you'd like."

Visibly irritated, he replied, "I don't know what you're talking about."

I leaned back in my chair, curious to see how long the conversation would last. Mom spoke more confusing phrases, and this annoyed him even further.

"I have no idea what you are saying!" He shook out his napkin violently and placed it in his lap. Mom smiled benignly.

They served a toasted cheese sandwich to the woman across the table. She peered at it through smeared glasses slid half-way down her nose. "Thank yew, thank yew, thank yew," she chanted. Then she took her potato chips and arranged them delicately on top of the sandwich, like she was working a jig-saw puzzle. She ate neither the chips nor the sandwich. When she stood up, an aide came over urging her, "Why don't you stay in your chair and try taking a bite?".

But the woman only patted the aide on the shoulder and changed her refrain. "Bless yew, thank yew, thank yew." Afterward, she navigated between the tables and wandered off down the hallway.

Mom watched the woman depart and then pushed out her own chair.

"Stay here, Mom. They're about to serve lunch."

She looked at me pointedly and answered in a firm voice, "There is no elephant on my plate."

"I think it's chicken, Mom. I think they're serving chicken for lunch."

I don't know why I attempt to keep some fragile thread of the conversation intact, trying to bring logic into nonsensical conversations. It didn't work, anyway. There was no convincing her to stay at the table. While the rest of the residents enjoyed their lunch, we went outside.

When the clouds drifted out of the way, the sun was warm on our faces and the breeze felt soft against our skin. I walked with her in circles, listening to the airplanes as they crossed overhead. At one point she held up her hands, "Wouldn't it be wonderful if he'd come down from there?" She looked at me with a wistful, innocent expression. She was speaking about her father again.

～

TODAY I FOUND Mom asleep in her bed with a lavender stuffed bunny that made its appearance around Easter. This was an addition to a pink fuzzy pig whose origins are unknown to me. Clothes, towels and shoes, all unfamiliar, would routinely mix with her own belongings. A visiting Boy Scout troop could have dropped off gifts for the residents or there was a mixup in the laundry room. The concept of possessions is lost on Mom, so I try not to let myself get too carried away figuring out what is hers anymore.

An aide explained that Mom slumped over the table and had to be returned to her bed. Just tired, they assured me. I crept around her room, watching her breathe and touching her cheeks. She looked peaceful, and I didn't notice any signs

of illness. I debated waking her up so we could visit, but depriving her of sleep sounded like a bad idea.

When I walked toward my car, the wind caught my hair and rippled my shirt. I felt like I'd been let off the hook, released from jail early. My heart leapt at the unexpected stolen time I would use to catch up on my other responsibilities. A small voice inside my head whispered a question: When did taking care of my mother become a burden?

*She decided to free herself, dance into the wind, create a new language. And birds fluttered around her, writing "yes" in the sky.*
— Monique Duval

My niece died suddenly and this devastating circumstance had a surreal feeling to it because no one will tell Mom that her granddaughter is dead. There's a possibility that the news wouldn't register, the conversation would be meaningless and Mom might walk away prattling about some odd topic. Or, like the rest of us, the loss would bring her to her knees. And what's the sense of that?

When I returned to the memory care, the logbook was peppered with comments about Mom "wanting to call Susan" or "wishing Susan was there". My chest hurt reading those passages. Sometimes I long for the day when I become anonymous and truthfully, I'm surprised it has not already arrived. She has trouble remembering how to use silverware.

I would think muscle memory would be more deeply engrained than the recognition of your daughter, but I guess emotional ties are stronger than the rote use of flatware.

～

WE WENT OUT to the courtyard to walk. The spring had been unseasonably cool, but it was a warm, lovely day. I helped Mom shrug out of her jacket, she's always cold, but she must've craved the sun on her skin too. The courtyard has a circular path and is surrounded by the building on three sides. It's not uncommon to see residents with their noses pressed to the glass, watching us, while we enjoy the open sky. The fourth side is a wrought-iron fence with a keypad operated gate.

Someone near the assisted living center keeps peacocks and installed a "Peacock Crossing" sign in front of the building. A peacock's cry is unusual cry and sounds like "EEE-Yowl, EEE-Yowl". Mom turned toward the noise, spread her arms out wide, and called back to that bird. I read that peacocks can be heard from a mile away, Mom wasn't quite that loud. I hope.

A visitor was sitting under the shade of the porch trying to make a phone call and I was tempted to turn around to see what he made of the situation. Fleetingly, I considered shushing her, but embarrassment is no longer part of my repertoire of emotions when it comes to Mom. Instead I marveled at how closely she mimicked the bird's call and I wondered if, somewhere nearby, a peacock thought he was about to get lucky.

Joining us in the small circuit was a man in a tattered bathroom and a woman learning to use a walker. The latter wore an orange vest with straps over her gym suit. The therapist gripped the straps, holding her upright as she leaned

forward, taking one cautious step after another. Her progress was slow.

All of us looked up at the jangling noise created when a staff member swung open the gate. The woman in the orange vest stared at the unbarred entrance for a second. She straightened her back, swung her body to face Mom and the robed gentleman, and hollered…"Run!" She pointed at the open gate for emphasis. Her voice was breathy with the exertion of her labors, but she wasn't giving up. "You can get out of here!"

The staff member startled at the shouts and almost dropped her bags. Once she'd appraised the situation, she threw back her head and laughed and laughed. Mom was delighted. She scurried to the giggling staff member like a child running toward her parent. I winced as she rambled across the uneven lawn, but she made it to her destination successfully and the aide embraced Mom like she was an old friend. The woman on the walker muttered as she passed by the still chuckling duo. "You missed your chance. You'll never get away now."

~

MOM BOUNCED with excitement at my arrival. She left her place in the half-circle surrounding a woman playing the guitar and made it to my side after bumping some residents out of her way.

"So happy," she said. The rest was unintelligible, but her delight was obvious. I'm not always sure she knows I'm her daughter. She rewarded her caretakers with the same greeting. She reminded me of Mister Rogers, always throwing out compliments like: "You are pretty!" or "Such a nice, nice lady".

The woman who followed Mom to my side leaned over and whispered, "She's been having hallucinations all day."

I can take a lot—there's always been drama in the medical world. But hallucinations are not my strength. Years ago, when I was an intern at a children's hospital, a mother brought her child into the emergency department for hallucinations. With eyes as big as saucers, she climbed up her mother's body, shrieking in terror. My training included broken bones, wheezing, lacerations, and seizures. Not imaginary biting insects. I'd never turned away from a crisis—but that day I ran. I found the attending doctor, explained the situation, and together we hurried back to the room.

"Bugs! Bugs!" the little girl screamed, "They're biting me!"

That doctor slammed her hand down on the stretcher and in a loud voice announced, "I killed them!"

The girl collapsed into her mother's arms. "Thank you," she whispered.

My mom wasn't seeing bugs, apparently she was seeing a man. In the middle of a long winded, one-sided conversation, she looked over her shoulder and announced, "Oh, he's gone now." Gave me the shivers.

∼

TACOS WERE A TERRIBLE IDEA. I knew that, but I also remembered how much she liked them. We navigated toward the counter to place our order. I called out our request while swatting her hands away from pieces of chocolate cake encased in see-through plastic containers. *Why did I do that? Who cares if she has chocolate cake for lunch?* It was my upbringing. Ultimately, it's her fault I think you have to eat some form of nutrition before you indulge in cake.

We made it to the table after I tugged her away from starting a conversation with an older gentleman. He kept

glancing at me and frowning during the rest of our lunch, and I suspected he considered me quite rude to pull her away like that. But I don't know what to say when mom babbles her gibberish, interjected with scattered recognizable words.

At first, the polite listener will lean in with a puzzled expression on their face. They ask her to repeat what she just said. She will ignore their request and prattle off more nonsense. Their eyes will widen, and they'll look to the side for an escape route. I get it. I try to avoid the inevitably awkward encounters.

The lettuce, tomato and beef were already on the table, her lap and her chin. Eating tacos is a messy business, and it's far worse if you forget how to hold it correctly. But she's happy. Very chatty. She pointed to the window, a nearby table, a light fixture and explained something to me. In gibberish. I nodded when it seemed appropriate and smiled at her most of the time. I rearranged her hands around the taco and reminded her to take sips of her soda.

When we finished, we made the slow shuffle to the door. Along the way, we passed some speakers strung up on the ceiling. A woman's voice, singing a Mexican ballad, flowed all around us and mom cocked her ear to listen. She turned to me with a questioning look and commented, "I don't understand a word she's saying."

I smiled back at her, but said nothing. *I know the feeling*, I thought.

THE NORMAL LOT was full today, so I parked in the rear of the building. My path toward the front entrance took me past the courtyard and I could see that Mom was outside. She flashed me a smile like I was Santa Claus and then she ran toward the gate. Well, it was kinda like running. Have you

ever seen a toddler pretend to gallop like a horse? That's what she did, galloped past the man in his bathrobe holding onto a cane. Skirted around a woman asleep in her wheelchair with her mouth dropped open. She's amazingly spry for her age.

She slipped her arms through the fence and attempted to hug me through the iron bars. "Are you taking me with you?" she asked.

I hadn't planned on any outings, but how could I turn her down? We drove through McDonald's and I ordered her customary hamburger and chocolate milkshake. She laughed in glee when she peeped into the bag. I drove to a nearby park.

"Look at the nuns," she said, pointing toward the small pond. Gliding across the water was a dark gray momma duck with her ducklings in close pursuit. Mom stood up, pointing out the flight pattern of a black bird darting back and forth over our heads. A squirrel nibbled on an acorn just a few feet away and a woman walking her yapping dog waved at us from a distance. When the breeze blew a strand of hair across Mom's face, she pursed her lips and puffed it away, then rolled her eyes and made a funny face.

She finished the burger, but it took our combined effort to keep the bun in the correct position. When I handed her the milk shake I'd hidden from view (to encourage her to finish her lunch) she smiled broadly and said, "I love that color."

I love chocolate too. I've read articles about how therapeutic it is. It can lower inflammation, decrease your stroke risk, reduce the risk of diabetes and improve your mood. Mom once caught me on a rough day when I was in medical school. "Do you have chocolate?" she asked. "Don't be afraid to use it."

I give my mother sweets quite often. There's some

research that suggests a potential link between poor diets, high in sugar, to Alzheimer's. But it's too late to worry about such things. Neither of us worry about a lot of things we used to. Sunscreen, for instance. Mom was religious about covering her pale face with the highest sweat-proof SPF she could find. A pink wide-brimmed hat was her trademark. One skirmish with melanoma and she considered the sun her mortal enemy. But no longer. She tilts her head back and the sunlight washes over her face. She's got freckles that I've never seen before.

Not everyone understands. I just called her doctor, annoyed when they informed me of her *slightly* elevated cholesterol. They'd drawn her blood without telling me—she was probably scared, and for what purpose? There is absolutely no reason to change her diet at this point.

When mom grew restless, we walked back to the car. I'd been listening to Celine Dion's *The French Album* and mom swayed with the music as it poured from the speakers. And then she started singing along…I don't speak French, and neither does she, but she sure sounded convincing. It was a marvelous day.

13

*Do You really Want to Hurt me?*
— Culture Club

It was a horrible day. She strode toward me with a grim, disturbed expression and then took my arm and guided me toward her room. Once there, she paced back and forth, spewing out her grievances. None of which I understood. There's always this shadow of recognition in what she says. Phrases pop out from the bizarre, illogical one-way conversation like "hurt me" and "he's a bad man" and, with more emphasis, "need to leave now!"

I felt helpless. Nothing in the logbook helped me interpret her behavior. I wondered if she was tired and encouraged her to lie down. She glared at me and mumbled "don't understand". I agreed with her, and she was pacified for a moment. When I offered her donuts, I received a lot of garbled accusations that I took to mean: *I am an unfeeling, clueless, ignorant daughter.*

I listened to the flow of more words that make me sick. "Grab me" and "hold me down" and "not going to let him". My conversation was lighter as I attempted to distract her from her dark mood. "It looks like a pretty day," earned me a sideways expression of mutiny. I tried: "I can hear them making breakfast, would you like something to eat?" With that question, she folded her arms over her chest, thinned her lips, and narrowed her eyes.

When a staff member with bad timing walked in the room, Mom faced the woman and sneered. Enunciating every word, she told her "You're not going to…" She left the sentence unfinished. The worker shrugged nonchalantly and replied, "I'll come back later."

"Huh!" mom puffed out, victorious at the woman's exit. But then she grew even more hostile, and I had no idea what to do. She paced the room like a caged animal, slammed her hand on her dresser, tugged the blankets from the bed and scowled at the pile on the floor. Glared at me. Paced more. This went on and on and nothing I said had any impact.

It had been a tough couple of weeks, and I wasn't at my best. I watched this furious woman, bearing no resemblance to my mother, trash her own room with my chest tight and my stomach queasy. I knew there was a possibility her agitation would continue to escalate and then she'd attack me. I resented the unanswered questions, the chronic fear that she'd been mistreated, the worsening of the disease and her emotional swings that couldn't always be explained by pain, hunger or lack of sleep.

"If you're allowed a bad mood, then I am too!" I spat out. And then, regretfully, a parting shot, "I'm leaving."

Mom turned stone-faced. Her words drew blood when they struck my back, "Do you want me to just die?"

~

They'd chosen a soft gray-blue color to repaint the memory care, and I walked down the halls admiring the color and wondering what mood she'd be in. When I didn't find her walking around, I grew apprehensive. I held my breath when I opened her door.

She was sitting in the sole chair in the room with a blanket wrapped around her despite the warmth of the memory center. Somehow, in the forty-eight hours since we'd parted, she collapsed within herself. She was slight, fragile. Broken.

Her eyes met mine, and a whimper escaped her mouth. A lone tear slid down her face. I fell to my knees in front of her chair and she bent forward and allowed me to wrap my arms around her shoulders. She spoke in broken sentences. "Sorry, sorry, sorry." Followed by a hoarse, "Came back....you came back."

I cursed this disease that never ceased in its relentless attack on her brain. It stole memories of her family, impaired her ability to use silverware, and robbed her ability to dress or even toilet by herself. Yet, somehow, it preserved our argument in her consciousness?

"Sorry. Love you. Hurt you. Sorry, sorry."

I cried. Why did God allow her to keep this one memory from a million others lost to her illness? What cruelty was this?

And far, far worse...How could I have walked away from her?

~

You'd think you'd get used to it, but you don't. Every time paramedics are called to the assisted living center, I assume it's Mom. A broken hip. Another bad spell.She slipped in the shower. She stopped breathing. My breaths get choppy and

my gait quickens. It's not until I pass by the room where the staff are gathered that I slow. I can see the edge of a stretcher, but can't make out what is going on. I'm ashamed of my relief.

Mom was in a really good mood. She hugged me and chattered her nonsense. I nodded and tried to answer her when she looked at me expectantly. I'm always listening for anything in her garbled talk that might mean she is hurting or scared or tired.

She had a new helper but the woman wouldn't meet my eye. I didn't know if she's shy or if I should be suspicious. Mom hugged her before she departed, a full body hug that took the woman by surprise. Mom leaned back before releasing her and said, "You're beautiful." The woman stoically accepted the hug, but when Mom said those words, that woman's face lit up. I guess she's okay, I don't know that I'll ever trust anyone with her again.

~

THEY'RE STILL PAINTING the trim in the memory care and now they're replacing the carpets. I wondered if the ladders and worker's presence would affect Mom—I got an answer pretty quick. She bounded off the bed when I walked into the room. With her once dark hair and petite form, she reminded me of an elder version of princess Leia. The transmission was garbled, but I could make out some words: "protect yourself" and "watch out" with a stern warning that it was "best to get out of here".

With every noise outside her room, her eyes found mine. The pounding of the hammers, the scraping of the concrete, the jangled metallic sound of a ladder being repositioning and worst of all... masculine voices. She looked half-fearful, but also half-triumphant, as if she'd been proven right. She

spent the better part of an hour keeping me appraised of the danger we faced.

At one point she passed me a small prayer book and asked if I wanted to see it. "It's a child's book," she said with disdain. Years earlier, I took my mother to watch a remake of *The Jungle Book* movie. I'd wanted to take her to the movies, but most were scary, violent, or so complex I worried she wouldn't enjoy it. When I heard her sing along with a song, I considered our outing a success.

Afterward, she questioned me, "Did you like the show?" I read her eyes; she recognized I'd taken her to a child's movie because she was declining. Even now, when she's paranoid and can't remember which shoe goes on which foot, she knows the difference between an adult's and a child's activity. I'm sure she's forgotten about the movie, why can't I?

∼

IT SEEMS heartless to tell Mom when I'm leaving town, she has no concept of time to know when I'll return. I check the camera frequently when I'm away. Sometimes Mom wanders around the room with no purpose. She'll walk up to a wall, stand quietly, and then pivot around to smooth the sheets on the bed. Or I may catch her dressing—putting a shoe on, and then pulling it off, and putting it on again. Once, she shadowed an aide tidying up her room. The aide guided Mom to a chair, and then Mom and I watched the woman strip the sheets from Mom's bed.

Mom started vomiting the day before my departure, and the memory care unit couldn't find her liquid anti-nausea medication. There was a lot of rummaging around, and they finally produced a pill. I'm fairly sure it came from another resident's medicine drawer and I had mixed feelings about the situation. It was the same emotion I had when my

precious daughter would come home from daycare with a diaper labeled "Mark" in bold blue marker. Slight disapproval that they'd borrowed from another diaper bag, followed by a lot of gratitude that she wasn't "bottom naked" as my son used to say.

She was holding down liquids and eating by the end of the day, so I kept my travel plans. Mom stayed in bed for the duration of my trip. She told my sister she was "going home" to see her mother and father. My sister believed Mom was giving up. I believe my grandfather gave up. But was it possible, at her stage of dementia, to make a decision like that? Or was she sicker than I realized? Not sleeping? Medication change? (surely the new doctor wouldn't....) Had the Alzheimer's caused her to slide down another step, and this was our new normal?

My throat thickened on my sister's comment. Is she is giving up because we are not visiting enough? Is she lonely for her family? I missed one of our visits—did that upset some balance? I decided to talk to the aides and double check her medications. Again. This carnival ride doesn't end. Her disease is relentless, and my anxiety for her has no boundaries.

14

---

*Games People Play*
— Alan Parsons Project

*M*om opened up her arms for a long hug when I arrived. Her eyes were moist, and she had a worried expression, so I scrambled to find something to occupy us. Fortunately, a man I've never seen before called out an invitation to join him in a new game. He had a sales-man's voice and wore a shirt with a logo I didn't recognize. Mom and I joined the circle forming around the Ringmaster.

He held a pink polka dot balloon, and he tapped it in Mom's direction. She pushed it back, and I congratulated her. She smiled softly and took my hand in hers.

The man next to me concentrated hard on the air-filled orb's trajectory. He raised a blue-veined hand to prepare for the balloon's arrival and then, after a successful tap, he tipped his head in response to the accolades of the crowd.

The next woman's gray hair was smooth and shaped attractively around her benign, congenial face. She has a permanent half-smile that reminds me of a baby-doll. The new activity intimidated Dolly. Her touch was light, tentative, and the balloon spun like a ballerina's pirouette in mid-air before the ringmaster snatched it to continue the game.

Her neighbor was slumped over in an armchair taking a nap. The Ringmaster called her name just as the balloon arrived in front of her face. She awoke with a startle, swatted aggressively, and the balloon sped back toward the center. It came with such speed that instead of moving on to the next player, the Ringmaster reflexly slapped it back. It flew back and forth. The napper alternated her hands, looking like a boxer giving punches, until a noise from the side distracted her and the balloon floated to the floor.

The Ringmaster scooped the balloon up and pushed it toward the next player. Her wide eyes give her a perpetually startled expression, and she only used one arm during the game. I suspected she had a stroke, but her coordination and handling of the balloon was admirable. Her jaw was tight when the balloon descended toward her, but she relaxed and smiled after a successful hit.

The next player has advanced Alzheimer's. She's been known to repeat a phrase over and over and over again. "I'm not going to eat that. I'm not going to eat that. I'm not going to eat that." She speaks in a monotone with no expression on her face. One day her phrase of the day was "You are ALL CRAZY!" When the balloon came in her direction, she winced and raised her hands in self-defense.

A newcomer joined our circle, and this Diva wore an abundance of mismatched jewelry. The gems on her fingers (she's got more than one ring on each digit) sparkled when she reached for the balloon. Her manicured hands grasped

the toy when it floated in her direction, and she smiled widely. She held the balloon up like a trophy, and the Ringmaster had to remind her to return it to the center. From that point on, she tried to keep the balloon each time it came her way.

The Ringmaster changed the game by tying another balloon to the first. *What madness is this,* I think. As you could predict, when hit, the balloons careen and tumble in the air like a moth flying in a random pattern. I leaned forward in my chair waiting to see how this crowd will react, but they are up for the challenge.

Mom hit the balloon, and it flew wildly to the right. She immediately apologized, but the Ringmaster grabbed the balloons and pushed them back toward her, reassuring her that everything is "just fine". The Ringmaster had trouble controlling his creation too. He swiped at the balloon, and it flew at my neighbor. The man released his hold on his cane, spiked the balloon like a volleyball, and called out "Have mercy!"

The startled-looking woman's turn again. She successfully tapped the balloons, only instead of floating back toward the center of the ring, one of the balloons burst in a loud pop. I held my breath, but the Ringmaster was quick to reassure everyone. The man next to me declared in a loud voice, "I believe I've soiled myself." He smiled, and I thought he was joking, but it's hard to know for sure.

Our circle grew. It took some time for the next woman to get her legs up on an adjoining chair, but then she was ready. With the addition of more balloons, now two pink polka dot and two blue polka dot, the movement of the balloon mass was less erratic. This made me feel better. Life in the memory care has always struck me as mercurial—the resident's moods, their health, the turn-over of the staff. I'd like

something I could rely on around here...like a toy that travels a straight path. The new player had a sense of humor and when she caught the balloons, she stuck out her tongue. The ringmaster opened his mouth in mock shock and she pushed the balloons back to him.

Dolly may have been intimidated in the first round, but she pushed the balloons back more aggressively on her next turn. A men shouted, "Well done!" but her half-smiling expression didn't shift with the compliment. The sleeper had to be woken again, but her reflexes were cat-like. She swatted the ball successfully back to the center and closed her eyes again.

The Ringmaster declared the game a victory, and the participants clapped for themselves. They passed out half-filled water cups, and the woman in the wheelchair drained her cup and called it delicious. She took a long finger, ran it down the length of the cup and then licked a droplet off her fingertip. Next, she tilted her head back and held the cup upside down over her mouth, like a toddler waiting for the last dribble of ice cream. I'm so caught up watching her, I failed to notice Mom has finished her water too. She's proud of her empty cup.

Mom walked me to the door when the time came for me to go to work. Once there she had some parting words for me. "Kind of a little bit of a look for the apple side." I repeated the words in my head, searching for meaning, but came up empty.

~

YOU GET to know the names, faces and even room decor of the residents when your entertainment is walking endless circles around the unit. On one walk, Mom motioned to a

door and then pointed to the name plate beside it. "That is my *last* husband," she declared.

My eyebrows went up. The Farmer was continuing his flirtations with the female residents of the memory care. My sister watched the man run his fingers through my mom's hair. He took her arm in his and they strolled down the hallway together...leaving my flustered sister behind. I'd heard of elderly romances and always wondered how I'd react if it happened to Mom. The Farmer held her hand and made her smile. I welcomed him to our imaginary family.

~

MOM SAT in one of the chairs forming a circle for another game. She gave me a perfunctory smile, but broke eye contact quickly. The aide pointed me out when she thought Mom didn't realize I had arrived. Mom turned obediently and gave me the same empty smile.

The new Cruise Director was thin, energetic and prone to laughter. I liked her immediately. She set up three plastic bowling pins in a triangle and she handed a beach ball to the first woman. The Diva, wearing three shirts and a random assortment of jewelry, accepted the ball graciously. Maybe she's always cold like Mom, or maybe she just prefers abundance in everything. She knocked down two pins, and everyone cheered.

The next player in our game has a Southern genteel accent, fashionably styled white hair and an *unlined* face. I looked at her hands and neck for any evidence that she's older than I am, but by the end of my inspection, I still can't tell. Suddenly I'm frantic to scoot my chair backward and remove myself from this circle.

It's not uncommon for staff members to remark on how much I look like my mother. I'm flattered because I think

Mom is beautiful, but I also get a little sick to my stomach. *What else have I inherited from my mom?*

～

HE LOOKED the part of a country western singer with a brown felt hat positioned level on his head, pearl snaps in a line down the front of his shirt, and a yoke with an elaborate embroidered design. When he smiled, lines radiated from the sides of his brown eyes. No rookie, the entertainer knew how to coax a smile from the grumpiest members of the audience. Singing his ballads into a wireless microphone, he wove between the chairs, making eye contact with each of the residents. He knelt in front of the man with the uncombed hair and an oxygen tube running from his nose. Shook his hand firmly, as if they were friends and greeting each other after a prolonged absence, and then refused to stand again until the man grinned reluctantly. With the women…he was a touch flirtatious.

He'd pat their shoulders, slide his palm down the length of their upper arm, rest his larger hand on their age-spotted, smaller ones. If they didn't smile right away or refused to make eye contact—he'd whisper something in their ear. I'm not sure what he said, but it sure melted the ice. Their gazes would follow his movements for the rest of the show after that.

Mom didn't need a lot of coaxing when he approached her. She pulled herself upright, taking perhaps longer than she had in the past, and started waggling her hips to the beat of the music. She shook her head, clapped her hands (sometimes in rhythm and sometimes not) and slid first to the right, then the left. When he offered her a hand, she twirled underneath his arm, and then giggled and almost lost her balance.

For a few minutes I was lost in the music too. I tapped my feet to "Great Balls of Fire" and laughed out loud at Mom's made-up dance steps. More residents and staff gathered, and they followed Mom's tango/two-step/boogie, laughing at her expressions and clapping at the conclusion. Mom stole the show.

15

---

*If you've got nothing to dance about, find a reason to sing.*
— Melody Carstairs

*M*om's vacant eyes held my own. She hadn't been in bed when I checked at 5am, so there's no telling how much sleep she got. Not much, if her pallid face was any indication. She struggled to get to her feet when I held out my hand, then walked hunched over, like she was in pain. Her speech was even more fragmented and confusing than usual.

I removed her shoes with some difficulty, worked to force her rigid body down, and adjusted her quilt. She was asleep within seconds. When her breaths lengthened, I took a few steps backward, but she sensed the movement and sat straight up, looking anxious and disoriented. I pushed her back down, murmuring instructions to close her eyes, and then returned to my silent post by her bedside.

When my daughter was a toddler, I'd stand over her crib

until her eyes shuttered closed and I was convinced that she was asleep. Any wrong move, a scuffle of my shoe on the carpet, the intake of my breath for a yawn...her eyes would flash open, she'd pop to her feet and hold out her arms to be picked up. More than once, I dropped to my hands and knees and crawled from her room.

Mom's door squeaked when I opened it. I winced, but kept walking when I didn't hear any noise behind me. Mom was missing out on the fun. The Ringmaster was back, and he tossed a bundle of tied up balloons to the Diva. She'd dressed up for her performance, the purple feather in her headband coordinated with her wildly colored capri pants. When she shoved the balloon back, her sequins sparkled.

~

MOM SCOOTED OVER, allowing me to sit next to her, while the entertainer of the week plugged in his equipment to prepare for his performance. Her eyes had that dewy look you see at airports when families get reunited. In between the gibberish and pointing, she asked, "How are you?"

She nodded at my response, but I'm not sure she knows who I am anymore. She refers to "Susan" in conversations, not recognizing that our thighs are touching and it's me that buttons up her sweater when I touch her hand and find it chilled. It doesn't hurt like I thought it would, maybe because I haven't completely disappeared yet.

Dolly had a tray on her wheelchair and she fisted a piece of cake. Crumbs fell from her too tight fingers. Her eating was not in dainty nibbles; she awkwardly shoved the entire square toward her mouth. She managed to get some of the cake between her lips and she looked around with interest as she chewed. When the entertainer sung "The Light of the Silvery Moon", she closed her eyes and swayed to the music.

Margarita slept in a wheelchair behind me, and a U-shaped cushion kept her head in place. I haven't seen her walk in a long time, and she's sleeping more and more.

The Captain smiled when the music started. Straight-nosed and ruddy-cheeked, he's always wearing a stocking cap over his bald head, reminding me of a fisherman. I'm still not sure he has dementia, but the thought of choosing to live in the locked unit to be with his wife (who clearly does) is too much for me to fathom. His normal uniform is a sweatshirt over athletic shorts, showing off his muscular arms and legs. He was probably a weight-lifter or gym junky, but I always picture him securing ropes, adjusting sails and brawling with the sea. When he saw me singing and swaying next to Mom, he gave me two 'thumbs-up'.

During "I'm looking over a Four-Leaf Clover", a worried-looking guy stood up. He took shuffling steps to the woman working the medicine cart and complained that he still hadn't gotten his money. He seemed satisfied by her assurance that she'd look into the matter.

Dolly meticulously inserted her left-over crumbs in the narrow slit between her sleeping neighbor's shoe and sock. The Cruise Director caught me watching the precision with which Dolly accomplished her task. Her eyes widened when she recognized what was happening, but then she shrugged her shoulders and smiled. The threshold for action is considerably higher here. Learning to float on top of the current, instead of fighting the waves, is my new goal.

"The Jail House Rock" made Dolly forget her crumbs, and she shimmied her shoulders and tried to get out of her chair. The cushioned tray, designed to allow her to rest her arms and hold things (like a piece of cake), prevented her from standing.

"Whoo-hoo!" shouted a clapping resident, energizing the entertainer. The Diva, wearing a straw sun hat and a velour

sweat shirt jacket, enjoyed the music too. One of her multiple necklaces didn't quite fit over her head. When she turned to watch a housekeeper carrying a mop, I could see a line of glass pendants shimmering across her forehead.

At the end of the entertainer's act, two women entered the memory care. Mom struggled to get to her feet, but they arrived before she could get upright. The women were dressed conservatively in crew necked sweaters, chino pants, and sensible shoes. Their name badges identified them as church representatives and the first one asked, in a heavy accent, if Mom would like Communion. Mom nodded. In a trio of quiet feminine voices, they murmured the Lord's prayer together. "Our Father, who art in heaven..."

Mom knew every word. Every. Word.

Afterward, she accepted the small wafer in her mouth and holy water from a perfume sized vial was rubbed on her forehead. They moved on, weaving between the walkers and cushioned chairs, generously sprinkling their holy water on all the residents. This took me by surprise, I've known the Catholic church to be particular with their Communion. I'm not sure how Mom qualifies anymore since she can't attend confession. They splashed the blessed water without restraint or concern that it might land on a Baptist or even an atheist.

I couldn't believe Mom was able to recite the prayer—it must be engraved in her head after decades of devotions. I thought about other sentences in her repertoire, also hard-wired from frequent use.

"How are you?"

"How is your family?"

"You are beautiful." This one catches people off-guard. She once said it to the lady collecting the trash in her room and the lady flushed bright pink and scooted backward,

forgetting to return the trashcan. She slid the empty container through the door several hours later.

All of her rote phrases focus attention on someone else. Except for one phrase: "I love you." That's my favorite.

~

HOW IMPORTANT ARE BRAS ANYWAY? I did a subtle hug, felt for the straps against her back and found that Mom not wearing one. In the past, Mom would have been mortified at being in public without this undergarment. Now I'm the one that's embarrassed.

I once read a study that said bras do nothing to relieve back pain or prevent sagging. One researcher said that breasts would have more tone if we *didn't* wear bras. Even with the knowledge, I can't fathom my mother going without a bra.

Mom looked good. We walked around the courtyard and she pointed out plants and chairs, spoke mostly gibberish, but would occasionally throw in a lucid statement. "You've lost weight," she said with sympathy. I glanced down and wondered if she was right, I hadn't noticed any change, but I had cut down on my sweets. Eating an amount of chocolate correlating to the brutality of the day wasn't the best idea.

I'm endlessly questioning how much of mom's communication has meaning. Would I understand her better if I spent more time with her…like a mother instinctively understands her toddler's prattle? Was I missing anything important?

During my reflections on this topic, Mom's conversation flowed into a new topic and her hands shook in agitation. When she pointed, I realized what disturbed her—a row of tiny ants trailed across our path from one landscaped bed to another. I stomped on a few, and once the threat was over, we continued our walk.

I read the journal of Mom's daily activities out loud, skipping sections describing her agitation or paranoia. She smiled when I asked if she enjoyed the chocolate ice cream shake (it's not uncommon for her aides to bring her treats). Today, they noted the discovery of her brown bear in a kitchen pantry. This good news was followed by a distressing, "The purple bunny is still missing!"

It was a brief visit. We walked arm and arm down the hallway, and I hugged her frequently along the way. Usually, I have no trouble slipping out the door, but she took me by surprise when she attempted an escape behind me. I jerked the door shut and watched her eyes fill with tears on the other side. I wanted to yank her out, but then what?

I turned my back on my mother. Inhaled slow breaths through an aching throat and willed myself not to sob out loud. When I peeked over my shoulder, her face was no longer pressed against the glass. Perhaps she wandered away, distracted by a noise or a picture on the wall. Or maybe she'd collapsed at the foot of the door and was crying like I wanted to.

Bras…they're not important.

*After silence, that which comes nearest to expressing the*
*inexpressible is music.*
— Aldous Huxley

*M*y day started with visions of homemade blueberry pancakes and hot tea. By the time I finished my shower, the texts started rolling in.

*Mom is agitated this morning and tried to choke another resident.*

*The other resident's neck is all red.*

*The memory care is going to file an incident report.*

There was a time when the first text would throw me into a state of dazed denial. I'm past that. When I was a child, I smirked when my mother gave me spankings, her blows to my bottom were symbolic. But this is not the woman that raised me, and she is more than capable of inflicting harm to any resident or caretaker who gets in her way. I remind myself of the atrophy of her brain, the plaques and tangles

preventing her nerves from talking to each other, but in times like this, I almost believe in demonic possession.

None of us know the implications of an incident report. Could she be kicked out of the memory care? Forced to remain in her room?

Her aggression didn't improve through the day. Despite my wish to be a calming presence, to soothe her when she's angry, I wasn't successful the last time...or the time before. More often, I become one of the threatening monsters in the nightmare she's living. It's painful to see her when she's like this. It made no sense to go to the memory care.

Maybe genetic imprinting made me get into the car. *I have to help my mother.* I'm pulled by forces stronger than my ability to detach from the situation. *Soul ties.* Abused children do this. They defend their parent's anger outbursts, lie about the bruises that stain their little bodies. They fight like little tigers when social workers separate them from their abusers.

I played my husband's style of rock music as I drove. Loud. Pounding. I gripped the steering wheel and tried to keep visions of my mom's angry glare from my thoughts. Reconciling this woman and the mother who raised me is getting harder and harder. I used to dread the day Mom would forget who I was, but that's just the lousy hors d'oeuvre in this feast.

The surrounding cars are like fish darting underwater until I blink my tears away. *I am strong. I can do this.* When I arrive, her eyes are mutinous, she allows my embrace, but does not hug me back. She's not pacing—so that's a good sign. The aide pointed out a minor cut (perhaps from when she flung a coffee cup?) yet to be cleaned and bandaged.

No one could explain what started the outburst. Like her Alzheimer's, her mood swings are often idiopathic, a term used in medicine to mean *we don't know*. I tried to get her to bed since sleep deprivation has a solution, but she looked at

me suspiciously when I attempted to remove her shoes, resisted when I urged her to lie down. After a lot of pleas and negotiations, she put her head on the pillow.

Just as she relaxed, an aide came in the room and mom jumped to her feet with a speed that surpassed her age. She narrowed her eyes at the newcomer, drew her hands into fists, and her entire body started shaking. Anger? Fear? I hugged her, hoping to dampen or extinguish the angst, but I accomplished nothing and she remained stiff in my arms. Mom reluctantly allowed the aide to place a bandaid on her injury. She paced the room, her agitation escalating, and I reached out to my sisters for help.

When I clicked on the link my sister sent, Mom lost her fierce scowl and cut short her restless patrol of the room. "Be Not Afraid", a song played regularly at her church, calmed her quivering, slowed the relentless picking of her sweater. She stopped jumping at insignificant noises. Apparently, music does soothes the savage beast. I wanted to hug my sister. When the song ended, I clicked the replay button. On the second round, Mom called out a word or two of the lyrics and then, like the gears of a bike engaging as you switch speeds, she started singing in a low, mournful voice that reminded me of Etta James.

The hostility drained from her body, leaving behind a fragile shell with Mom's face on it. I helped her to the bathroom when she motioned in that direction. She didn't wait until she reached the toilet, but pulled her pants down in the center of the room and then shuffled toward the commode. After a lot of hesitation and false starts, she plopped down. I tried to take off her shoes (to remove and replace the disposable briefs) but she decided she wanted to pull her pants up again. I had no idea if she peed. Getting her dressed again was a game of Twister and involved some contorting moves on both of our parts.

I got her tucked in bed after some confusion about the sheets. Perhaps the top sheet should be a different color, so it's more obvious? Next, a quilt of white blocks with pink borders. It's an antique, and should've been wrapped in tissue and protected in a box. But its familiarity brings comfort to Mom, so we watch as the threads come loose and the pieced fabric design unravels a bit more from the thrashing it receives from the washing machine.

On top of the quilt goes the Christmas fleece. It's blue with fat black penguins wearing striped candy-cane colored hats. "It's her favorite," her aide told me once as she helped tuck it around her lower legs. "My feet are cold," Mom mumbled before closing her eyes and drifting off.

I snuck out of the room, cursing myself for not bringing some WD40 to fix the squeak in the door. I let my breath out when it's obvious the noise did not disturb her.

On the drive home, I realized that I was craving a warm chocolate dessert with gooey caramel.

*I want to die.*

I should go shopping and buy something extravagant... maybe a new dress, with shoes and jewelry to match.

*I want to die.*

I'd like to be in Italy, sitting at a bistro table, sipping on a glass of white wine, with a travel itinerary in my hand. Watching the sun strike the condensation on my glass.

*This will never end.*

*Still Crazy After All These Years*
—Paul Simon

S andwiches are more technical than you'd guess. Schlotzsky's is one of Mom's favorite places to eat and we go often. I search for ways to reach her and since eating is such a primal instinct; I have this fantasy that she'll take a bite of the sourdough bun and the taste will trigger a memory of one of our previous trips here. She doesn't know how to hold the sandwich together.

I coach her, but when I turn my back, she'd separated it. She concentrated on the half with the meat, nibbling on the black olives and then turning her hand over to take a big bite of the bread. Her right hand holds the squished second half of her sandwich, but she's blind to its existence. Toddlers do this. They clench their fists around a cookie and then forget to eat it.

Pediatricians screen children to follow their milestones:

assessing their ability to string three words together, hop on one foot, or brush their teeth. Alzheimer's is a backward study of the developmental chart.

When we returned to her room, I helped her to the bathroom. The skin around her bottom was fiery red, and she winced when I wiped her. An infant's diaper rash presents no angst on my part, but I know nothing about maintaining hygiene in a woman with Alzheimer's, a woman who can't complain or verbalize pain. Are there better wipes or creams? I'm always looking for answers to the assortment of problems that is our daily existence.

She put her arm through mine when the time came for me to leave, intent on escorting me to the door. Her gait was lopsided, probably because one of her shoes was lying abandoned on the bed. I sat her down, slid the shoe back on, and realized she'd pulled off the other shoe as I worked on the first. I have to work faster, this disease feels like it's crawling all over me. Once all articles of clothing were in their appropriate place, I pulled her to her feet and we strolled to the door. Her good mood was a victory of sorts.

～

MY MOTHER WAS NOT in bed at two in the morning when I checked the camera. At four o'clock, she was pacing the room. Pulling out a drawer. Closing a drawer. Picking up a book and moving it across the room. Smoothing a sheet with her hand. Starting all over. At five o'clock, the room is empty and I know it will be a rough day.

I found her clutching a marker in front of an adult coloring book. Her page was clean, but her aide made considerable progress on her own picture. Mom's voice cracked with emotion and she was weepy, so I hustled her into the room and make for the bed. She'd passed some crit-

ical point in her exhaustion, and she twitched relentlessly. I spoke to her in soothing tones, rubbed her shoulders, and pushed the hair out of her eyes. She chattered non-stop. I remembered the music, pulled out my phone and clicked the link. *I've got this.*

When the church hymn started streaming she sat up in bed, wild-eyed with excitement. She looked around the room as if searching for something…or someone. "Do you HEAR that? God is HERE!" She whipped off her blankets, shoved herself out of bed, and disappeared out the door.

≈

"I've been meaning to talk to you." The Cruise Director met me at the entrance and I'm instantly on guard. Had there been more problems? Would they toss her out? When we passed by another employee, the Cruise Director gave her the eye. "This is Judith's daughter," she said, her words thick with meaning.

*This is bad. They've put together a team to deal with it.*

She touched my arm, stopping me in my tracks, and my mind spun with possibilities. I wasn't sure if Mom hit someone, gotten sick, had another spell, or…if she'd died. Surely, they'd call me for that, and not wait for me to show up?

"We're thinking of taking your mother on a special trip."

"Huh?"

"Your mother really enjoys seeing airplanes, and we thought we'd take her to the airplane museum."

They're sweet. They'd noticed her fascination with planes and wanted to do something special for her. The Cruise Director shook her head when I explained why she was enamored with aircraft. Even the professionals fall down the rabbit holes.

~

THE CAPTAIN and his wife strolled toward the dining area. Instead of harpooning whales, it looks like he's recovering from a different battle. An oxygen tank adorned his walker and clear plastic tubing looped over his ears and traveled under his nose. He walked slower, but that didn't stop him from talking to the staff.

"How are you feeling today?" The aide placed vinyl placements, water glasses and silverware at their customary table.

"Much," he paused, leaned heavily on the walker and took a big inhalation, "better." His wife had the napkin in her lap before he could make it to his own chair. "Not as much coughing."

"Chicken and scalloped potatoes or beef with broccoli?"

"Beef," said in between panting breaths.

"And your wife?"

"Chicken." He's got a determined look on his face, but he needs another breath before he can continue. "She doesn't like beef."

His wife said nothing, nodded politely when the food was served.

The Captain may have some physical challenges, but he's still taking care of his wife.

~

"IT SURE IS STICKY OUTSIDE." Mom and I stepped outside for a stroll, and the muggy air proved her right. Puddles crept onto portions of our walkway and the petunias bent their heads in submission to the thrashing they took the night before. When Mom started tip-toeing, I realized she wasn't talking about the humidity at all. The storm had washed

mulch onto the concrete path and she was avoiding the 'sticks'.

Earlier that day, a man stood in the living area meticulously dabbing powdered makeup on one of the female residents. I watched for a moment, but then continued down the hallway. Another question unanswered. I noticed that one of the woman always looked 'made up'. It took me months to realize the dark lines along her lashes and the rosy color of her lips were permanent tattoos. For the most part, the residents in the memory care are beyond vanity. Well, except for the Diva.

At lunch, I sat next to a woman who's celebrating her birthday. She's a Faded Flower wearing neon colored beads and a headband with the words "Happy Birthday" in pink sparkles. When I congratulated her, she smiled and nodded energetically. The birthday girl leaned forward to bring her mouth closer to the plate, ignoring her utensils and her hands. Mom tapped my arm and glanced meaningfully at the woman, who looked like she was playing a game of bobbing for apples. It always amazed me when mom pointed out, with an eye-roll, someone who had slipped further down the curve than she.

As a result of her latest tilt toward the plate, the Faded Flower's crown slipped into her pureed food. She stopped eating, got a stricken look in her eyes, and opened her mouth to say something, but no words came out. I gave the cardboard a quick wipe and her tiara was as good as new. I worried the headband might be too tight, but she grinned and resumed eating once it was perched on top of her head.

Mom folded her napkin into a tiny square and then hid it in her closed hand. It'll likely join the others in her room. She's got quite a collection of them.

*Shine on You crazy diamond*
— Pink Floyd

*M*om smiled and reached forward in her chair to hug me. "It's been a good day," the aide said, "a good week, in fact." Mom's camera had not been working and I'd been antsy. With the aide's words, I felt some stress slide from my shoulders.

More women arrived to the table, some shuffling and others rolling in their wheelchairs. A man wearing a pressed button-down shirt and khaki pants approached the gathering. He looked familiar, but I couldn't place him. The Cruise Director was gone, he explained, and he would act in her place until the new hire arrived. He gave more assurances, but I'm pretty numb to the staff turnover. I hope that the Cruise Director is happy wherever she ended up.

I liked new guy and found him friendly and engaging. When the Diva arrived at the table, he called out her name,

and she smiled graciously. She wore a sequined headband under her hat and he looked puzzled by her sparkly accessory, but said nothing. Her lipstick was brighter than usual, a vibrant fuchsia color, and her fingers were loaded down with at least a dozen rings. Since the weather had chilled, she's taken to wearing a knitted gold colored blanket draped over her back like a shawl.

He distributed colored pencils and a paper with a simplistic flower. Mom tried to fold the paper like her napkin, but I straightened it and handed her a tangerine-colored pencil. She knitted her brows together, tightened her grip on the pencil and started moving her hand over the paper. The pattern was random, her pencil marks had no relationship to the image in the paper. She lost interest pretty fast.

When I toured facilities searching for the right place for Mom, one center framed drawings by Alzheimer's patients. They were placed sequentially, labeled with the duration of the illness, and it was disconcerting to witness their decline in the artwork. Sadly, Mom's drawing would be at the far right if I were to nail it to the wall.

Mom dropped her pencil when the music came on. She closed her eyes and moved her lips in what appeared to be a silent prayer. Her eyes popped back open at the conclusion of "Jesus Loves Me".

The new man told fascinating stories involving the Jonas brothers, selling expensive wines, and identity theft. The Diva commented on each tale. When the Brit came to the table, a charming lady with an English accent, I was caught off guard. She had perfectly lined red lips, a hint of blush and artistically shaped eyebrows. "He did it," she explained, pointing to the new guy. The Make-up Artist was dismissive of the compliment, but you could tell that he was flattered his work has been acknowledged.

~

LAST WEEK I got a mailer from the local recreation center. You know the type, brochures with images of energetic people swimming, playing basketball, or taking dance classes. Guess what? The Farmer was in one of the pictures—I'd recognize that movie-star smile anywhere. Did he sneak out of the memory care and attend evening classes?

Our camera was still not functional, despite attempts by my sisters to fix it. I lie in bed at night feeling like I've forgotten to lock the doors.

~

MOM PLAYED with a piece of grated cheese from her salad. Her caretaker greeted me and then pointed out the new stemmed glassware on the table. "Are they serving them wine?" she asked me. I laughed, but then realized she was serious.

"You know...to get them to sleep faster?"

A server interrupted our conversation, "Lemonade or cranberry juice?" It was always the same options. I'm not sure which I found crazier—serving alcohol in this unit or any variation from the liquid options.

Mom and I were sitting at Dolly's table. Mom leaned forward with bright eyes when the server puts Dolly's plate down."Ice cream," Mom said, pointing to the plate of pureed cauliflower. Dolly dabbed her finger into the white mush and afterward held out her hands, as if repelled by the smear of the food on her digits. Her helper snagged her hands under the table.

The Diva was fashionably late for lunch. The sequined band circled her hat instead of her forehead and when she walked by, a mixture of lavender and baby powder wafted

across our table. I made a mistake when I pulled out a chair for her at the adjacent table.

"She needs to sit somewhere else." A woman in a brightly colored muumuu explained to me, "She took a pile of dirty clothes and put them in my room!"

The Diva looked offended. "She's mistaken," she said with a sniff.

"I'm not mistaken. You did it three times, and I kept asking you to stop." She held up three fingers for emphasis. "When I raised my voice the last time, you got upset."

"I did not get upset."

"There you go again. Getting upset." She leaned back heavily in her chair and then looked at me with an arched eyebrow.

The server arrived with a plate, accurately read the situation, and then guided the Diva to a new seat. Peace was restored.

Mom's helper put a piece of broccoli on her fork. Halfway to her mouth, it tumbled off, rolled over her thigh and then landed on the floor. Fork still in hand, Mom leaned over and said, "Bye-bye!" She kept her eye on her neighbor's pureed cauliflower.

Mom only ate about 20% of her food. There, I did it. I've documented the percentage of her food intake. I'm not sure why it's important. What would I do if she stops eating all together? The helpers write these percentages down along with chronicling her number ones and twos each time she goes to the bathroom. I think recording these facts gives the illusion that you have the situation under control.

Mom's helper, a woman with naturally curly hair and an outgoing personality, put another piece of broccoli on Mom's fork and then informed me about her recent diagnosis of breast cancer. She opted to forgo chemo in favor of

some tea from the rain forest that she's purchased from Mexico because it was cheaper. I wanted to shake her.

"I'm too old," she explained. "I wouldn't do well with chemo."

"How old are you?" I blurted out. My rudeness didn't faze her.

"I'm 58." She sounded apologetic as if, somehow, she waited too long to get breast cancer.

"You are not too old." I insisted. People like this make me nervous—believers in tree barks and teas. Remedies with no studies in medical journals to validate their use. Where did medicine go wrong that people are searching out pixie dust for their cures? She'd already explained that she'd had a surgery at the Mayo hospital. "You need to call the Mayo and talk to them about your concerns." She didn't look convinced. "Please," I urged.

Dolly's caretaker was listening in. She held a spoonful of pureed food to Dolly's mouth but Dolly refused, tightly pressing her lips together. The caretaker used the edge of the spoon to pry Dolly's lips open and pour some food in her mouth. Most of it dribbled down Dolly's chin. Both of them looked rebellious, and I wasn't sure if the caretaker was as distressed about the cancer treatment plan as I was, or if she was having a rough day with Dolly. Dolly shook her head vigorously when the spoon returned.

Speaking of the caretakers—I love reading what they write in the journal. One of my recent favorite entries: "… then we danced in the Alzheimer area. I'm not a good dancer, but I tried because Judith loves to dance." Yup, that's why I am so grateful for these women.

She was in a great mood. Laughing a lot. My heart felt glad on days like this, the same pleasure you get from watching a puppy scamper and trip across the floor, listening

to your son enthusiastically describe his new job, spying on a woman as she delicately kisses her newborn.

On the way out, I stopped by the front desk to ask why it looked like someone took a weed-wacker to Mom's hair. They explained they'd hired a new hairdresser.

*Those who were seen dancing were thought to be insane by those who could not hear the music.*
— Friedrich Nietsche

om's helper whispered an update before the woman with a guitar slung around her neck started the show. I hoped the church hymns would help Mom's somber mood. The woman across from me had a round face, thick arthritic fingers and a sweater that had seen better days. Her appearance and disposition shouted *I'm a grandmother and proud of it*. A wreath of gold, purple and crimson mums adorned the front of her walker. More floral branches shot out, like bursting firecrackers, from her hand rests. It was ambitious, and I wondered how many seasons the family would keep up with the display.

In the middle of "Amazing Grace", I realized the woman in the recliner was not breathing. Her head lolled to the side,

and her mouth gaped open. The v-neck sweater, stretched out and low cut, revealed a good portion of her chest wall. There was no movement. One, two, three. I counted slowly, wondering what I'd do if I got to twenty and she still didn't take a breath. Jump up, drag her to the floor, and start rescue breaths? It seemed kinder to look away and let her soul pass on quietly. As the singer's voice swelled to "Twas grace that brought us safe thus far…" the woman sat up in the chair and gasped. Definitely not dead.

One lady glared at the entertainer during "Rock of Ages". The skin around her eye was swollen and bruised as if she got into a fight. More likely, she tried to get out of the wheelchair without help. Dolly ignored the music and looked away from me instead of smiling. It looked like no one was having a good day. When a man wandered into the circle and blocked the view of the woman wearing a muumuu, she told him sternly, "Sit down so we can all sing!" He froze at the command, and then spun in a circle with a flustered expression on his face.

"Sit down!" the woman insisted.

The guitar player put down her instrument and helped the man to a chair, eyeing the complaining woman the whole time. Muumuu lady had a disgruntled expression on her face and she crossed her arms over her chest.

"You're a teacher, aren't you?" The guitar player stood in front of the muumuu'd complainer after successfully navigated the man to a seat. "Teachers just can't help instructing and guiding others." The complainer nodded her head and looked pacified.

It didn't sound like instruction to me, more like a cantankerous demand. Teacher's presence in this locked ward confused me. She had more of her faculties than any other resident. She read the newspaper, had conversations with the

aides about politics, and at mealtimes she instructed her dining companions on the proper utensil to use. Did someone lock her up? I would be fuming mad if I were trapped in here.

I looked back at Sleeping Beauty to make sure she was still alive. She was.

The Diva tapped her toes to the music and made comments that I could understand like: "My mother taught me this song."

Behind the group, a pajama-clad, unshaven man slipped out of his room with a calendar in his hand and a mission. He looked satisfied when an aide pointed to the right date and returned to his abode. A moment later he cracked the door open, looked out at our group with suspicion, and then slammed the door shut again.

I sat cross-legged in front of mom's chair, and her fingers played with my hair. I'm always rubbing her back, patting her shoulders, kissing her cheek, but I can't remember the last time she's touched me like this. It felt good.

WORK HAD BEEN BUSIER than usual and skipping my visit to Mom was unbearably attractive. After days of rain, the sun was shining and I could sit on my patio, stretch out my legs, and hope for a touch of color. But I know what a dangerous slope looks like. How one skipped visit, with a series of excuses, can expand to multiple. It's frightening how seductive the urge is to give up. You tell yourself that it makes no difference—she doesn't really recognize me anymore.

She was paging through a magazine, but stood up to greet me with her arms wide. *She knows who I am.* We walked hip to hip with my arm slung around her shoulder and her hand

around my waist. She chattered, smiled, hugged me tighter, then chattered more. *She loves me.*

The sunlight made her happy, and she started jumping like a child with an imaginary jump rope. Rotating her hands by her side and leaping in rhythm to music only she could hear. Her jumps took her backward, too close to the concrete edge, and I flattened my hand against her back to prevent a spill. Mom took that as a signal to change her moves.

She tilted her head up, raised her hands as if to worship the blue sky and then took a larger jump. The Diva was enjoying the weather with us. Sunlight sparkled on her jewelry, and her sunglasses followed Mom's movements. Mom's last jump caught her attention.

"You'll fall if you're not careful."

Mom switched from jumps to swinging her hips and pivoting in circles.

The Diva chuckled. "She's a good dancer, isn't she?"

Mom overheard, she demonstrated an impressive shimmy and then a random hip-hop move. *Show-off.*

~

THE FARMER WAS DEAD. I hadn't seen him for a few days, but that didn't strike me as unusual. When I passed his room on the way to Mom's, I saw the nameplate was missing and the room was empty. He appeared in good health and I jumped to the conclusion he'd moved to another memory care. The aides told me a different story.

"He hated to shower…" The woman stood behind a counter, cutting meat into small pieces on the plate in front of her. "Some of them do. They give us a lot of trouble." She moved the plates to a row on the counter for the servers to distribute. "One night, he just got undressed and climbed into the shower, all by himself. He put on his best outfit and

got into bed. They found him like that the next morning." The woman stopped speaking and stared out the window for a second. "He was a good one. Your mom liked him a lot."

*I know*, I thought to myself; *he was her last husband for a few weeks*. I have mixed feelings about the passing of these men and women who share the same meals and tread the same carpet as my mother. Before I become familiar with their quirks and habits, I recognize their journey ends here, and their existence has been condensed down to several stained shirts, rumpled pants and comfortable slippers. Gone are the dirt-encrusted garden gloves with a hole in the index finger, the dining room table with chalky water rings, the toolbox, tennis racquets and travel brochures held together with a rubber band. What's left behind is the stooped posture, cackling laughter and bad hip. My peephole into their lives has the film of dementia on it, their images are indistinct, a nebulous form that began dissolving before I put my eyes to the door. Their deaths offer no surprise or shock.

~

MY SISTER FIXED THE CAMERA. Mom's bed was empty at four o'clock in the morning. Sometimes it's best not to know.

~

THE TEACHER SAT at the bingo table, looking over her reading glasses as if getting ready to give a lecture. The Diva pursed her cherry red lips and followed the progress of the family touring the facility. The Captain studied his card with his forearms resting on the table. Bingo has never interested Mom and certainly not now.

When I realized how cold Mom's hands were, we went to her room. It was a comedy trying to get her fleece jacket on.

She put her hand into a pocket instead of the sleeve and it was downhill from there. Hand into the wrong sleeve. Hand into the right sleeve, but immediately pulled out again. After more twisting, contortions and giggles, she finally had her jacket on.

Still flush with her accomplishment, Mom pointed to the framed picture on her bureau. "Who's that?"

The breath whooshed from my chest. It was a picture of Dad. I'd handled her inability to recognize me as her daughter, but the erasing of Dad was another matter.

"It's Jack."

"Jack, Jack…Jack." She sang his name and giggled more. "Where is he?"

*If I say he's dead, would it make her sad? Would she mourn a man she doesn't remember?* I had no idea. "He's not here," I answered lamely.

"Well, where is he?"

"I don't know." I was walking on a minefield. I realized it would be best if she didn't remember him, didn't experience the loss or the loneliness after his departure. She shrugged her shoulders at my response and launched into a string of gibberish. I read the aide's journals while she picked up a blanket and moved it across the room. Nothing new to report, the same ups and downs in mood, the percent of each meal that she ate, and remarks on her bowel movements.

"Shake Your Body" by the Jackson Five played in the living area. Mom held out her right hand, shuffled a step to the side and then swung her hips. She repeated the move on her left. I stared at her, fascinated by the spontaneity of these dances. She raised her eyebrows and made a face as if to say *watch this.* Her moves became more exaggerated.

An arm elevated with a flourish.

She spun in a circle.

I imitated her actions, and her grin widened. She became

the teacher, slowing her movements so I could replicate the roll of a hip or a sideways step. Down the hall we danced. Me, slightly self-conscious. Mom, no longer encumbered by any need to be demure. My reserved, timid mother is gone, and this new being has taken her place. She laughs impulsively, abandons her meal in favor of the dessert, and dances whenever the mood strikes her.

*"Music is the moonlight in the gloomy night of life."*
— Jean Paul Friedrich Richter

*A*nother aide made a comment about my resemblance to my mother, and I feel like I have a target on my forehead.

One to two percent of Alzheimer's cases will be *early onset*, usually defined as before age 65. Familial Alzheimer's is caused by a genetic mutation and if one parent has the disease, fifty percent of their children are *destined* to have Alzheimer's. Sporadic cases of Alzheimer's are more common. In those cases, certain genes increase the likelihood, *but not certainty*, of getting the disease. The APOE genotype e4/e4, for instance, is associated with a 30-50% chance of dementia by age 85.

I listened to a story on the radio about a cloned bull. Despite the hopes of the owners, and the identical genetic profile, the new bull was not the same as the original sweet-

tempered animal. A dislocated shoulder and near goring experience proved it. Just because I look like Mom doesn't mean I'm destined to have the disorder. Studies show that other factors play a role in whether I will get Alzheimer's. I'm counting on exercise, diet, and sheer bull-headedness to spare me from this affliction.

∼

THREE LADIES WERE on the sofa taking a nap. The first one's head was angled funny, and I wondered if she'd wake up with a sore neck. The last one had a tee-shirt on that read *I Need Coffee*.

Mom approached me with tears in her eyes, and her arms open wide. "He's gone." she said. Her body quivered when I hugged her. Without loosening my hold on her, I looked over her shoulder and tried to determine who was missing. She was grieving for someone, but who? Did another of the residents die? Was it Dad she was missing? Grandpa? Her next husband—the Farmer?

Did it matter who? *I couldn't fix this.* I took her outside, pointed out planes, urged her to touch purple-tingled shrubs, encouraged her to remember the Johnny Cash song that streamed overhead. Nothing worked. Her eyes remained red-rimmed and weepy.

We returned to her room where I sat her on the bed, slipped off her shoes and helped her lie down. She squeezed her eyes shut and pulled the blanket up to her face, longing for the oblivion of sleep. The photograph of Dad on her bureau reminded me of how much she craved an uncon-scious state after his death. I snuck out when her soft snores ruffled the sheets, congratulated myself on not letting her mood get to me. Perhaps this had nothing to do with anyone dying, perhaps this was some random misfiring in her head

—it would've been foolish to react to her emotional state. *Float on the current*, I reminded myself as I headed to the car. When a sad song came on the radio, my eyes filled and I admitted that it didn't matter whether someone had actually died. When she hurt, I hurt.

~

THE NEW ACTIVITY director flashed a smile at me when I sat down next to Mom and then continued the game. He reminded me of a professional football player. A thick gold chain circled his neck, tattoos ran the length of his bulky biceps, and a dark du-rag covered his head. On a white board, he'd listed large animals in a colored marker. Already on the list: bear and gorilla. Mom wasn't capable of partici- pating, she kept busy telling me a story or reciting what she had for lunch. Who knows? He questioned the residents, and with a lot of prompting, he added lion and shark.

He added "Mmm!" under the next category—foods that smell good. A woman in a green flannel shirt stood up and shuffled toward him until her nose practically touched his broad back. I worried he might take a step backward and accidentally knock her down, but he was light on his toes for a big guy. He slipped to the side, took her arm, and escorted her back to her chair.

Responses for this category included peppermint sticks, potato salad, and chicken. They're random answers that wouldn't have made my list, but the Football Player was energetic and encouraging. At this point, I realized that the aides were walking around and whispering answers into the resident's ears. That's when he turned to Mom and asked about a new category: *Birds.*

I was ready. I whispered, "Say peacock, Mom".

"Peacock!" she blurted obediently.

"Yes!" He pointed his finger at Mom as if she was the star student, and I'm oddly proud of her when he added the word to his list.

The Diva heard the word peacock and sat up straighter in her chair. "They're right outside my window!" she bragged and then looked around the circle for a response.

The Football Player waved his hand to get her attention, "Can you name a bird?"

The Diva answered energetically. "Peacock!".

"That bird is already taken," he reminded her.

The Diva looked disgruntled. "But they're outside of MY window!"

"Right!" he answered. He twisted to address the woman sitting next to the Teacher, and she's hesitant in her reply, "Red bird?"

The Teacher didn't approve. "I don't think that's a type of bird, that's a color of a bird." She tapped her cane on the ground to emphasize the point. "Maybe you mean a Blue bird? That's the name of a bird."

The Football Player took her suggestion and wrote Blue bird on the board. It was the Teacher's turn next, and she offered a Mynah bird. She had to call out each letter for the Football Player so he could add the bird to the list. I didn't know how to spell it either. Afterward, the Teacher leaned over to her neighbor and gave her a suggestion. Flamingo went up on the board.

The Teacher's seat mate grew more confident. She waved her hand wildly, and when he pointed to her, she shouted, "Red bird!". The Teacher said nothing, but frowned and crossed her arms over her chest when he added red bird to the list. I looked it up when I got home. The Teacher was right, there is a species of bird called the Bluebird, but no red bird. And who knows how to spell Mynah bird correctly? How did she get locked up in a memory care?

∼

"WANNA SEE MORE?" She was in a fantastic mood. She rose from her chair outside in the sun and started dancing. When a bird whistled, she scampered across the courtyard to locate it and then whistled back, making elaborate arm movements and looking back at me with wide mischievous eyes. When it flew away, she pouted and dropped her head.

She was as manic as I've ever seen her and I laughed at her funny expressions and how quickly she went from one activity to another. She ran to the fence, shook the bars and clapped at birds overhead. Danced a jig. Did jumping jacks with a hip roll. More dancing. When the song "Jive-Talking" came on, she lowered the sweater from her shoulder suggestively...like a stripper.

"Oh my God."

She heard me, despite the fact that I'd muttered it under my breath. She frowned, as if disappointed in me, and said, "I'm not gonna do *that*."

*Did she know what I was thinking?* That she might be uninhibited enough to remove her clothes?

The Diva saw us through the window, and she came outside to enjoy the weather too. She still carries her purse when she leaves the room and is not as advanced in her dementia as Mom. She watched Mom's animated movements, and I wondered what she was thinking.

Mom put her hands on her waistline and took wide steps forward like a western gunslinger—a cowboy ready for a gun duel. With the next song, she pivoted on her feet and swung her arms—she's Chubby Checker doing "The Twist". It's exhausting watching her frenzied motions. Confusing and delightful. I gave up wondering what the Diva thought about Mom, I didn't know what to think.

~

"WHERE'S SUSAN," she asked as I helped her change out of her pajamas.

I didn't miss a beat. "I'm right here, Mom. Where's my mom?"

Mom's eyes twinkled, she grinned widely, and then laughed out loud. She tilted her head, touched her forehead to mine and peered at me over her eyelashes. She looked like she had a grand secret and she wasn't ready to share it. When she pulled back, I finished fastening her bra and slipped a shirt over her head.

She never answered me.

~

SHE TOOK a swing at my sister. Until now, I've tried to come up with excuses for her anger and aggression toward the staff and other residents. Admitting that she's been aggressive makes me sick inside, like I'm betraying her somehow. There's been a number of explanations put forth and I'm sure I can come up with more if I need to.

She'd been leery about a new resident. A woman with white spiked hair who walked around with a bag of her belongings asking, "Do you know how to get out of here?" The staff turnover continues to be high. Perhaps she's constipated. Her allergies might be bothering her. She's not sleeping well. For weeks, everything seemed good. Really good. Now this.

The staff assured my sister that everything was fine when she arrived that day—my sister makes a point of inquiring about Mom before she sees her so she can mentally prepare. Mom had enjoyed the tambourine music of a rotating performer earlier that morning, but something changed.

Mom was clutching a pillow and walking down the hall when my sister found her.

She called out to her, "Mom…"

Mom whipped around and screamed, "I DON'T KNOW WHO YOUR MOTHER IS. YOU ARE A HORRIBLE PERSON. GO AWAY!"

My sister tried to guide her back to her room, but Mom took a swing. When they made it to the room, the door was locked. I've not discovered an answer to the door locking issue. The staff lock the door to keep other residents out of Mom's room. I also suspect that they would like the residents out where they can be observed and kept awake so they don't wander all night. But I'm not sure.

Music was the solution, but it took a long time for it to work its magic. My sister turned the volume up and sung loudly along with the song. Inches from Mom's face. The way my sister described it, it sounded suspiciously like an exorcism. But it worked. God and the devil work in mysterious ways.

"I'm sorry," Mom told her, when the anger had been purged.

A friend asked me how this can happen. I described it like a loose electric connection…the slightest movement and the wires separate and the room goes dark. There's no telling when the light will go on again or for how long.

21

---

*After all, Ginger Rogers did everything that Fred Astaire did. She just did it backwards and in high heels.*
— Ann Richards

She had a lot to complain about. When I arrived, there was a flurry of activity in the memory care unit. Tables were being set up for a party, and the staff dashed around trying to organize the affair. I found mom sitting all by herself. She wore a soft gray sweater over black velvet pants. Someone must've retrieved the sequined black slip-on shoes from the recesses of her closet. I hadn't seen them for years. They'd draped two necklaces around her neck, one with alternating tan and white pearls and the other with large clear beads strung on a pale pink colored ribbon. Her hair was curled, and her nails painted. She looked adorable.

But when she caught sight of me and stood up, I read her face. It's the "I've got something to tell you and you won't like

it" expression. She spoke non-stop on the way to her room and my name was brought up frequently in her diatribe.

Susan's not called me.

*You don't have a phone in your room anymore, Mom.*

Susan's not visited me in a long time.

*That's not true. I come here several times a week. I haven't stopped.*

I don't even know where Susan is.

*I'm right here, Mom.*

She paced around the room, occasionally holding up something as if she'd found a pair of expensive woman's underwear in her husband's drawer. Her hand shook with the evidence of my wrong-doing. I tried distracting her by giving her updates on my kids, talking about the milder weather and asking if she'd enjoyed her breakfast. It didn't work. I offered to take her outside, but she ignored me. I tried one more time. "What do you think about the party, Mom?"

She stopped her pacing and stood in front of me with her hands on her hips. Her lips thinned and her eyes turned sharp.

"So you're in on that, too!" she accused, before stomping out of the room.

~

WHEN THE CAMERA image came into view, I saw scuffling on the right side of the frame. Mom wrestled with another person, and then fell backward onto the bed. I stopped breathing. She was closer to the camera now, so I zeroed in on her face. Her mouth opened, and I waited for a scream, but she laughed instead. The person outside the camera lens giggled too. "They're going to think we're crazy, you know that?"

Mom worked to push her arm through the sweater, a continuation of the struggle I'd witnessed. "Maybe we are." she answered.

~

DESPITE IT BEING NOVEMBER, the air was warm and the courtyard bright with color. Most of the year, the landscaped beds held oversized clumps of green shoots, but the ornamental grasses sprouted feather dusters in the fall. Delicate pink fronds on the Muhly grass and, through a trick of slanted sunlight, sparkling rows of glass beads on the hay-colored sprouts. Fairy grass.

Mom's face lost its tight intensity and something outside the fence stole her attention. She pointed at random objects and asked questions. (I realize it's a question when her voice goes up in pitch toward the end of a string of nonsense words.) Sometimes, she accepts my random answers. On other occasions, she looks at me like I'm the one speaking a foreign language.

She stepped up on the bottom rail of the iron fence, gripped the vertical bars with her hands, and leaned backward. The sun washed over her face, the breeze ruffled her hair, and for a moment she looked like a child on a swing. Eyes closed, floating upward, weightless. I wished it was always like this. Wished I could distill this moment and

bring it out so we might take a sip from the flask on bad days.

Voices from the parking lot broke the spell. She stepped down from the gate, picked up the pillow she'd abandoned earlier, and hugged it tight. "It's time to go," she told me. I felt a mixture of rejection and relief when I walked out that door.

IN HONOR of the Thanksgiving holiday, the Diva wore two hats. A straw hat with a wide brim covered up her usual hat. No glittering band on this hat, she's saved the bling for her necklaces and rings. Her bright pink lipstick traveled beyond the lines of her lips only twice. She sat in a half-circle watching a game show from the 1970s along with every other resident in the facility. Except Mom.

The Teacher, despite another bright muumuu, looked sullen. As I walked behind her, I saw her open up an envelope and pull out a card. One of those expensive cards with real ribbon and feathers in fall colors. The inside—I'd slowed down on purpose to take a peek—was completely filled with writing. In tiny, beautiful script. No simple "Happy Thanksgiving!" card. This was true correspondence. She'd already read it. I know because she glanced at it for only a second and then shoved it back in the envelope. She stared straight ahead after that, looking dejected, and I wanted to give her a hug.

I found Mom with her arms crossed over her chest and her teeth chattering. Her hands were like ice. I've noticed that care-takers dress Mom according to how they dress themselves. The woman on the early shift wore tee-shirts on days the frost covered the grass.

Along the way to her room, I recognized the clear beaded necklace hanging on a hook in one of the stations. This one

contains an array of purses and jewelry—colored plastic bracelets, golden chains with a variety of pendants, and a sundry collection of vinyl handbags. Cooking items were in the next center: an empty box of brownie mix, discount store pot holders, spatulas and over-sized spoons. A red and white checkered apron reminds me of Mom's *Better Homes New Cook Book*. It disturbs me to find one of these objects in her room, like somehow I'm responsible for Mom stealing from a display. I've returned the white handbag three times now.

While adding another layer to mom's apparel, I decided to take her to the bathroom. She was recovering from a bladder infection, and the mood swings that went with it weren't pleasant. It was harder than usual. I tried guiding her to the toilet, but she was distracted by a washcloth which she picked up and awkwardly tried to fold. And then a church bulletin, discovered on her bathroom counter, with a picture she needed to show me...

Once she spied the toilet and understood the plan, she pulled her pants down and shuffled across the room. She finally sat, looked at me with a comical face and said, "You might as well sit, this could take a while."

I laughed, but searched her eyes, wondering if she realized what she said. I overheard my grandmother trying to toilet-train my daughter. "Let's make some water," Grandma would say. Grandma would never use "pee-pee" like I did. If my daughter did not urinate right away, Grandma would encourage her to "push the button to make the water come out". My daughter would giggle and push her toddler finger into her belly button. I wondered what would happen if I push the button, but it turned out that there was no need. Mom started making water and then threw up her hands and looked at me with a proud smile. "Ta-Da!"

∾

FADED MUMS DROPPED their tired heads at the entrance to the facility. Fall was over, but no one seemed eager to remove them despite the approach of the next holiday. A sign in memory care said TODAY IS TUESDAY and displayed the countdown until Christmas. Mr. Complacent sat alone on the sofa, staring at a black TV screen, and listening to the piped in music. He clapped his hands, enjoying the rhythm of the seasonal classic. Grandmother strolled around with a walker already decked out with garlands of holly, creating a solid wall of festivity. Poinsettias burst from the greenery and swirls of red ribbon twirled around the legs like pepper-mint sticks. It's another strong statement. The Teacher read her book in a cushioned chair with her legs propped up and her cane leaning against the armrest. She smiled as I walked by, and her reading glasses shimmered in the sunlight.

Mom wasn't out with the others. The light was off in her room, and I tiptoed just in case she slept. The pink and white quilt, looking even more raggedy than last time I noticed it, was pulled up around her shoulders and her pale cheeks looked flushed.

"I think she's getting sick." The aide who trailed me into the room answered my question before I asked it. "She kept closing her eyes while we walked, so I figured something was up." The dark-haired woman nodded emphatically, "I know Judy and something's going on…"

*Her name is Judith*, I silently corrected her. She never liked the name Judy and someone who really knew her well would…the thought skittered away like a tiny beetle scur-rying for shelter. I didn't bother swatting any longer, it just didn't seem worth the effort.

This aide felt an attachment to my mom and I'm grateful for that. *Help me protect her*, I wanted to say, *from getting the flu, from curt staff members with deep voices, from loud music and*

*waving arms.* The list of what mom needs protection from is long.

We chatted in hushed whispers, and Mom slept through our conversation. I reminded the aide to call if she was worried about anything as I headed toward the door. Skipping my visit granted me some extra time to catch up with work, time I'd need if she got any sicker. My gait quickened at the thought of the havoc an illness might play on my already tight schedule.

Mr. Complacent was still in the living room, but he'd lost interest in the music. He'd pulled off all the cushions from the leather sofa and inspected the labels he'd found underneath with narrowed eyes, as if translating a secret code.

22

---

*The journey between who you once were, and who you are now*
*becoming,*
*is where the dance of life really takes place.*
— *Barbara De Angelis*

*I* found myself standing frozen and mute, in front of the cashier at Schlotzsky's. It happened like this….

I slept poorly. I compensated with extra cups of tea and topped it off with a latte. My weekend plans, the reward for unusually long work hours, were falling apart. I told myself it was no big deal and I could spend the weekend on the sofa watching Netflix. But I said it with gritted teeth.

I ran late to pick up mom. I'd promised to take her out for lunch the last time I visited and I don't trust her forgetfulness. She may not remember how many socks to put on one foot, but those sparks when the neurons connect occur at

random and unpredictable times. Her face fell when I failed to deliver on a past promise. Never again.

The white board sign announced: It's 20 days till Christmas! Mom stood up from the activity table when she saw me, leaving behind a pinecone and colored yarn. She greeted me in Chinese. Her words were frenzied with some stuttering thrown in. My breath caught in my throat. I wrapped my arm around her waist and she chattered non-stop as we walked toward her room. I'd never heard this speed of gibberish, and the alarming absence of a single coherent word frightened me.

My mind scrambled as we performed the necessary dance to put her jacket on. *Had she had a stroke?* The stuttering... she'd sounded like this when Dad died...back when we still spoke the same language. *Did something terrible happen?* I scanned the notebook, but nothing stood out. Alzheimer's is marked by stages, and I'd read that it can be obvious when they've made a transition from one to another. *Was that it? Had she taken another step down the ladder?*

She sat beside me in the car, buckled in, after the initial confusion about where to put one's head and arms within the confines of the seatbelt. When a song she recognized played on the radio, she held up her hands and played an imaginary piano as she looked out the window. Her favorite things are: purple pansies, ducks gliding on a pond, neon colored cars and waving flags. When something amused her outside, she looked at me with a silly grin to see if I'd gotten the joke. Halfway to the restaurant, her speech pattern reverted to normal, and then my smile matched hers.

We eat lunch at eleven o'clock and finish by the time the rest of the world swarms in from the parking lot. I avoid crowds. Their loud noises disturb her, and she flusters strangers when she stops to ask nonsensical questions. But I ran late.

She couldn't get into Schlotzky's fast enough. A Christmas tree, resplendent with white lights, generic red ball ornaments and haphazardly placed garlands of tinsel, stood next to the counter. She headed straight toward it. "It's beautiful!" she exclaimed with sparkling eyes and a gaping mouth. Then she held out her arms and twirled like Maria from *The Sound of Music*. There was no going under the radar from this point.

Next, she sprinted to the counter. "You are such a nice man!" she declared to the lanky uniformed teenager. He beamed. I find it odd that people will appreciate a compliment from a complete stranger. How would she possibly know if he's a nice man?

When she asked a question he didn't understand, he expected me to translate. Here's where it gets tough. I find it hard to interrupt her when she's talking because I've been taught to respect my parents. Silly, right?

I was flustered and trying to figure out what to order. We eat the exact same thing every time we're there, but when I opened my mouth…I said something completely different, and then had to correct myself. Meanwhile, she continued chatting. I didn't dare look at the cashier. He was young and he wouldn't understand. I assumed he'd be uncomfortable and avoid looking at her.

But he didn't. He nodded at her as if he understood everything she'd said, and then he smiled at me. He was asking what we wanted to drink when my throat swelled shut. It was too much—that expression of understanding or whatever it was. Too unexpected. I was blinking my eyes and trying not to fall apart in the middle of a fast-food restaurant. I ended up pointing to some cups and wordlessly handing him my credit card. She still hadn't finished talking. She'd seen the chocolate chip cookies, and she pointed at them with a hopeful expression.

I left her at the table when the buzzer lit up and it was time to retrieve the food. I half jogged across the restaurant, fearful that she'd stand up and wander away when my back was turned. But she was right where I left her, straining her neck to look out the back door toward the pond and hopefully, the ducks.

The meal was messy. I expected no less. She still recognizes the restaurant, the food, and the ducks, so we go regularly. Mom ate her sandwich with her eyes glued to the door. I saw nothing but brown twigs shooting up from the brackish water and I was worried that the ducks won't show. Focused on navigating her, I tripped on the step leading outside.

"Holy Mom!" she called out as she grabbed my arm.

For a moment, she appeared concerned about my near-spill, but then a flutter of wings distracted her. The ducks didn't fail us. She followed their progress as they glided across the water, and I did my best to keep her from spilling in.

On the way back to the car she told me, "I haven't seen Susan in a while." I was exhausted and instead of answering, I pulled her into my arms and gave her a big hug. Her eyes searched mine as she pulled back, and then her grip tightened on my arms. An odd expression crossed over her face and then, like a veil getting yanked off—my mom saw me. She recognized me. Her eyes filled with tears and her voice got hoarse. "Sorry, sorry, sorry." Her words were a plea for forgiveness and a knife to my heart. "I know you. Susan."

Do you know what is a thousand times worse than your mother forgetting who you are?

I do.

It's the grief and pain in her eyes when she realizes that she's forgotten her own daughter. I'm haunted by that day and I'm praying that she never recognizes me again.

*The music is not in the notes, but in the silence between.*
— Wolfgang Amadeus Mozart

om's aide was pulling out of the parking lot as I arrived. She rolled down the window for a quick chat.

"Is she in a good mood or…?" I asked.

"She's fine," she assured me, "a bit tired from waking up early. And she's had diarrhea, and it went all over the floor. She's okay now, though."

I haven't even made it into the building and I've already gotten a handful of impossible questions. *Is she sick? Did someone give her coffee again? Does she hurt?*

The white board announced "14 days till Christmas!". The Diva reclined on the couch with her eyes closed, taking a nap. A brightly colored red and green silk scarf, tied loosely around her neck, took the place of her usual sparkly neck-

laces. Her customary crocheted wrap enveloped her shoulders and her thin hand rested on a tin box by her side. I wondered what type of treat she'd received for Christmas... cookies? candy? or more jewelry?

Mom was lying in her recliner chair and woke when she heard the door.

"Hello, dear. Where are we going?"

I squatted by her chair, pushed the hair from her face and tried to see if she appeared ill. No flush stained her cheeks, her eyes were bright, and she'd asked a question that I understood. Maybe it was just the coffee.

I had no time to take her out and felt guilty despite her moving on to another topic. She waved her arms as she told me a story that involved Bluebonnets (seen in a painting we passed) and a chair. We do a lot of walking around the memory care. Lots.

My grandparent's upstairs apartment faced a park and Grandpa jogged on the sidewalk, looping the playgrounds and sports fields. Towards the end, Grandma stood on the balcony following his progress. "Joseph! Joseph, you turn around now. It's time to come back." She waved a red flag if her voice didn't do the trick.

I asked her once, "What will you do if he doesn't turn around and come home?"

"I'll get in my truck and go after him."

My grandma wouldn't let curbs or baseball fields get between her and her husband. I wish I had a truck that would bring me closer to Mom as she drifts away.

In the living area, we saw the Thinker, hunched over in a chair, concentrating intently on something across the room. Like a lot of Mom's clothing, her shirt shrunk and now the zipper running down her back rolls up and down like a sea serpent cresting the water. She didn't respond when I waved to her, and I'm not even sure she's blinking.

The residents sat at a table decorating construction paper to wrap around an oversized chocolate bar. Most had given up, but the Teacher still glued curly slips of colored paper to her design. Mr. Complacent alternated between pulling his chair forward and pushing it out. He made no progress on the project or his decision to leave the table.

When we passed by the craft area, I realized I'd not seen the Captain for a while.

You'd think I'd be used to it by now—the withdrawal of familiar faces. I've noticed that most assisted living centers prop a photograph of a departed resident in the building's atrium, accompanied by flowers or a poem. I made a mental note to check the front desk when I exit.

Beside me, mom swayed to the rhythm of a Christmas song she recognized. She grabbed my arm and pulled me away to show me a new dance move. A shuffle of bright blue sneakers, a twirl with one arm suspended like a ballerina. Her voice caught the familiar chorus, and she held on, uttering words and phrases that had been engraved in her memory. It was a good day.

$\approx$

DANCING IS MORE complex than you'd think. The frontal lobe of our brain, in its position behind our forehead, strategizes the slide of a foot or wiggle of a hip. The basal ganglia, deeper in the brain, coordinates our movements so we don't trip over our own toes. It's the cerebellum that allows us to keep a beat, to maintain the rhythm of the music. We understand some mechanics, but there is a lot we don't understand.

At one time scientists thought only humans responded to music. Dogs, cats and even monkeys could hear the music, but they didn't respond in rhythm to the song. Music might

soothe the savage beast, but he wasn't able to boogie to it. A scientist watching a video of a cockatoo kicking and dipping his beak in time to the music meant that dancing, synchronizing our body movements to music, wasn't unique to humans.

Dancing appears to activate portions of our brain that may help with stress, anxiety and even dementia. It releases endorphins, the 'feel good' chemicals in our body. I started reading about dancing when I realized how much my mom loves to dance—it makes her feel better. There is so much I can't do. I've not found a way to make her sleep better. I can't sit by her side for every meal, encouraging her to take another sip or bite. When she wakes up in the middle of the night, I'm not there to hold her hand. I'm frustrated by my inadequacies. But when the mood strikes her, at least she can still dance.

～

Mom rose in slow motion, like her body was moving through some gelatinous material. Dark circles rimmed her eyes and I couldn't tell if if she was waking from a nap or on the verge of falling asleep after a restless night. She probably didn't know either.

Her hair had been recently cut and curled, and despite needing a comb, she looked darling. She wore a red, v-necked sweater, and she was picking at the seam of a pair of new jeans with nails that held just a remnant of fuchsia. The aides painted her nails weekly, and it's something I'm not used to seeing. Manicures were not part of Mom's life. She's likely baffled by the strange colors of her nails, and she scratches the polish off as soon as her aide turns her back. One aide shook her head and said, "We should just do clear and then she wouldn't notice." I wouldn't count on it.

During the time it took to put my purse down, mom grabbed an Advent guide from her bedside table. She'd had a visit from a church representative again. Mom was always happy to see these visitors, but if anyone showed up with a clerical collar, Mom would swoon from joy. She stared at the words of the guide, her body facing the front of the room instead of where I stood, and she spoke nonstop. Her voice was monotone, the chanting of Latin prayers with some recognizable English words. I was invisible to her.

When she reached out her hands and offered the small booklet to the empty space in front of her, I realized she was hallucinating again. Her eyes were hollow, vacant. Wasn't it just a short time ago that the veil had lifted and she *knew* me?

I understood most of the words she used, but had no comprehension of what she meant to say. "I use the numbers and we go back to measure at the citigowat. Be there. Imagoas mayo cannot target. There is riceland no." She stared intently at the book, pointing out pages and taking a deep breath before starting each sentence. Her voice rose and fell like a minister at the pulpit.

The room smelled of smoke, and I wondered if someone snuck a cigarette in her bathroom. The idea distressed me only briefly. My observation that she was using less English and her sentences had more made-up words was echoed in the caretaker's notes. The aide also pointed out that after getting her hair done, "She's beautiful." I smiled when I read that.

Mom continued the gobbledygook, and *nothing* she said had any meaning. At least that's what I told myself. Because after Mom finished her dialogue and closed the book reverently, she looked up to heaven and whispered, "God help me."

MOM'S ROOM has transitioned into a child's room. A dark brown teddy bear is a permanent fixture on her bed and a floppy buff colored puppy, his companion. The latter has her name and room number written on the label attached to his hind leg. An odd assortment of old church bulletins, a 1970s book on travel, and a book featuring photographs of misbe-having cats is in her magazine rack. I don't see other rooms like Mom's. Most of these rooms have decor that's a flash-back to twenty, thirty, even fifty years ago. It's a reminder of how disparate this disease process is—everyone is forced down a different corridor of the maze.

She has fresh sheets, a child's pattern of pink unicorns, gray owls in mid-flight and orange foxes with upturned tails. Purple flowers are sprinkled between the woodland crea-tures. It's like watching her age backwards. She was a pre-teen when she carried her sparkly purse. Now she likes to sleep with the stuffed puppy, I'm okay with that.

THE FRONT DOORS have oversized wreaths amassed with wide candy-cane striped ribbons and white frosted bulbs. Christmas music greeted me when I passed through the entrance and the front living area was equally festive. A huge, expertly styled tree was next to the front windows, golden reindeer with a matching gilded sleigh graced the top of the mantle, and a bowl filled with holly and glass ornaments decorated the counter next to the sign-in book.

The woman at the desk nodded to me and then passed me a warning, "They have a stomach virus in the memory care unit." She fluttered her hands, "Up to you. You don't even have to go back there if you don't want."

As I walked toward the back, I imagined confused resi-dents puking in every corner. But when I turned the corner

—there was Dolly—sitting straight up in her wheelchair with a big smile. She acknowledged me with a classic beauty queen wave and then she and her helper disappeared down a hallway. Everything looked pretty normal in the unit. Mom sat on the sofa watching tv and the regulars milled around. An aide took the Teacher by her arm when she complained she'd lost her cane and they left on a quest.

Mom smiled at me, but didn't stand. I held back on hugging her since I recognized the benign smile she flashes at strangers. I'm getting better at reading her body language. Her aide wore a black Batman scrub top over a thermal long sleeve shirt. She noticed that mom was acting stand-offish toward me and she was quick to fill in the awkward space. "She's having a good day, but I don't think she's been sleeping too good."

I thought back to the times I've turned on the camera in the middle of the night or at five in the morning and Mom is not even in the room. No kidding, I'd be in a chronic state of hallucinations if my sleep schedule varied like hers.

*Moana*, a Disney movie, was playing on the television, but Mom's focus on the show was spotty at best. On one scene, Moana dived deep into the ocean to retrieve a glowing object. (I've not seen the entire show so I didn't know what it was, but the sound track reinforced the significance of the event) She surfaced with a dramatic flare and beside me, I heard clapping for her achievement. Margarita looked thrilled with Moana's accomplishment, but she closed her eyes and returned to sleep shortly after the event.

Mom ignored me as if we were two strangers forced to share a seat on the bus. As the aide and I chatted about our Christmas plans, she remained uninterested and uncharac-teristically silent. She used her finger to trace the image of Batman on the aide's shirt. When she declared it "Pretty", the aide smiled bashfully and replied, "I thought so, too." She did

stand up for the arrival of the church women. She greeted them warmly, accompanied them in The Lord's Prayer, which she chanted without error. Once finished, she turned and waved her arm in my direction. "That's my daughter," she said.

*All I Want for Christmas is You*
— Mariah Carey

Christmas morning started early. I wanted to make scones, but I didn't have the correct ingredients for any of the recipes online. I merged a few, pulling from my pantry the baking powder and flour. The eggs and milk from the fridge. I used to approach cooking, especially baking, with scientific precision. Actually, I approached life in the same manner. I believed that if I just followed the schedule, showed up on time, prepared for the crisis in advance... everything would turn out okay. I won't say I've given up on that lifestyle, but I've lost confidence that I was ever in control in the first place.

I added a little more vanilla to the mixture, used my fingers to shape the dough and then popped them in the oven. The scones turned a satisfying golden brown color, and it felt like an omen for the day. Mom and I'd shared

scones and tea in the past, and I needed to do this for reasons I don't understand.

The white board announced *Today is December 25* with a hand-drawn Christmas tree next to the date. Mom sat in a circle with other residents, wearing only a nightgown. Her face was blank when I call out to her. I told myself that she must've slept poorly, but it's hard to determine why she's better on some days than others. I squeezed her cold hand, helped to pull her out of the chair and we headed toward her room.

Along the way, we passed by four aides chatting at a table. For a moment, I'm irritated they didn't recognize her shivering. Shame replaced my irritation when I remember I'm not working while they're separated from their families. It's hard to blame them for slacking a bit.

The Diva was decked out for the holiday. A down vest topped the assortment of necklaces and a shimmering gold ribbon replaced the lace on her straw hat. As usual, rings flashed on her fingers. She paced near the door, waiting for someone to pick her up. Dolly smiled so big it made me laugh. She held a baby doll out for me to see and then drew it to her chest for a big hug. I can see what she got for Christmas! No sign of the Captain, but his picture wasn't in the front entry.

I changed mom into jeans and a sparkly silver top that reminded me of the silver strands of her hair. A long red cardigan and a Christmas scarf completed the outfit. It took a bit of time, but in the end she looked festive. She acted sluggish, so I pulled the log from the drawer to see if the aides recorded any problems. Some angry days. Some happy days. No clear trend, there hardly ever was.

She found the bag with the scone while I read the log. Smiled after taking a little nibble and then took a larger bite. Half-way through, she held it to my mouth to offer me a

taste. Even at this stage of dementia, she's consistently trying to share her food with me.

Maybe the scone triggered some memory. Maybe the vanilla and sugar wove some connection in her neurons. Her face became animated, and she bounced to her feet. She started jumping an imaginary rope, and her hands twirled by her sides. Crumbs flew in all directions, and she giggled at the sight. I wiped her mouth when she finished and we walked around the center arm in arm, admiring the decorations that had been present for the last month. She was in a wonderful mood when I left to go home.

My sister wasn't so lucky. Later that afternoon, I got a series of texts.

WENT AND SAW MOM. *Big mistake.*
*It was hell.*
*Even got her sedated, and it was still chaos.*
*She was holding on to the lamp, claiming it was God.*
*He IS the light.*

I'LL BE HONEST, I wanted to giggle when I pictured Mom clutching that lamp. My sympathy for my sister apparently wasn't strong enough to prevent me from seeing the humor in the situation. We've all been there with Mom, and we're getting better at dealing with the ups and downs.

≈

MOM HAD her arms clutched around a garage sale edition of a Betty Crocker cookbook. They'd curled her hair into a new flattering style and her nails had been painted too, a light pink color that complimented her pale skin. She'd scratched

the color off only two fingers so far. She walked slowly with her gaze directed on the floor, a weary soldier unsure of his destination.

I called out to her, but she didn't respond. She held her body stiffly for my hug, and grief swirled in her eyes when she looked up. For a moment, she searched my face, as if weighing whether I was friend or foe, and then she uttered two words...

"Save me."

The air whooshed out of my chest. I put my arm around her shoulders, turned her around, and in a slow shuffle we headed toward her room. Intermittently, she let out long sighs. Halfway to our sanctuary, she looked around frantically and said, "Where's Susan...where's Susan?"

I reacted impulsively, hugging her, and wishing I could cocoon her from her own madness. I tried to reassure her but received no response. The daily log didn't have any clues to offer, apparently it started as a good day: "Judith ate 90% of her breakfast, she loves danishes!"

I got her in bed, sent my sister a text and in seconds the link to her favorite church song was on my phone. Mom croaked out some words, and I kept hitting replay. In the middle of the chorus, she began sobbing uncontrollably. With the next repeat, she begged, "Oh God, forgive me. I'm sorry. Forgive me."

I didn't know what to do. I found it incomprehensible that Mom has ever done anything worthy of confessing. You might not believe me, but when we get to heaven, I'll point her out. You'll see—she'll be the one sitting next to the Virgin Mother. I was afraid to keep playing the music, but even more afraid to stop. I hit replay one more time.

She mumbled. Unintelligible words with a few pleas thrown in... "God, please, please... take me."

I switched to a song called "The Prayer" by Josh Groban.

Because after listening to her request, I needed soothing music as much as she did. I climbed in her bed, stroked her cheeks to wipe away the tears and then took her hand in mine. *When did her hand get so tiny and frail?* For the next twenty minutes she told me nonsensical stories, pausing in between tales to stare at the wall in stoney silence.

I assumed that she'd drifted off to sleep after a particularly long period of quiet, but she turned to me with clear, focused eyes and said, "It's time for you to go home". She looked completely lucid, like her synapses were fully functional, and my stomach clenched. *Does she know that she's alone? Locked up?*

I panicked. "It's going to be okay, Mom. Everything will be okay." I tried to kiss her pale, still damp cheek, but she turned her head away.

She whispered her reply as I walked toward the door. "I don't think so."

&#8767;

I CRIED ALL the way home. I swiped tears from my eyes at stoplights and worked to compose myself from imagined prying eyes in the cars on either side of me. But each time I put my foot on the gas, my eyes blurred and my breaths got choppy again. It was as if I was anonymous when I was moving forward and dreadfully exposed at each stop sign. Stupid. Ridiculous.

"Are you okay?" It was my sister on the phone, the one who'd forwarded the song. The one who rescued me.

"Umm…not sure." My throat was still thick from crying, and it was hard to hold a thought.

"I usually spend the rest of the evening in a fetal position on the sofa."

That was *exactly* how I felt, and the idea was tempting.

"It's not right hearing your mother ask God to take her. It's hard to listen to her when she's like that."

To be honest, I was afraid of the sofa. I laced up my sneakers and dashed out the door with twin hounds of torment and grief snapping at my heels. I feared giving into the sorrow, afraid that it would sap my strength in some inconceivable manner. I need to be strong. Even though I don't know how I can save her. Maybe I need to be strong so I can just be there. I don't know. I went for a run, gulping huge breaths of cold air and exhaling the anguish through clenched teeth. I can't give up yet. It's not over.

*The only way to make sense out of change is to plunge into it, move with it,*
*and join the dance.*
—Alan W. Watts.

They handed me a mask. They'd placed the entire building in isolation, trying to control another circulating stomach virus. Having dealt with infection control, I suspected that the gloves and hand-washing would do the trick, but I put their mask on and tolerate the suffocating sensation of breathing my own humid breath as I walked toward her room.

I was surprisingly calm considering I was responding to a text announcing more bruises. More allegations of abuse. I didn't have the fire of a righteous woman any longer. It's hard taking care of a demented patient. She's had hallucinations and she's had paranoia. She's been in vile moods, had manic giddiness, and was prone to spontaneous dances when

her favorite tunes came on. I don't know how much training these caretakers get, but I'm convinced that nothing can prepare you for this. I find it hard to get all noble and virtuous, to play the role of the conscientious daughter, when I can't imagine taking care of these women and men with their ever-changing moods and dramas. I walked into her room, dreading what I will find. Anger, bitterness, spite? Fear? Hysteria? No.

Inexplicably, it was a great day. She giggled when I ran the comb over her scalp and the static sent her hair shooting in all directions. She laughed when I washed her hands, never flinching when I gingerly touched the dark red and purple bruises encircling her wrists. There's no predicting what will happen anymore.

～

I FIGURED the odds of getting food into her mouth are about 25%. She's been losing weight and now I understand why. They'd delivered her lunch in a styrofoam container along with a package of white plastic silverware and a napkin that was woefully inadequate for a patient with dementia. One styrofoam cup held lemonade and another was filled with a dessert.

Chili was in a small section, penne pasta dotted with some herbs in the other. The largest section held the vegetable—okra swimming in a tomato sauce. It's madness delivering these containers to the residents, still quarantined to their rooms. The odds of them remembering how to open the lids, pull out the utensils, keep the styrofoam trays balanced their knees. It's the definition of insanity.

Mom didn't wait for me to unwrap the fork, but used a forefinger and thumb to retrieve a bean from the chili. I moved faster. She ignored my outstretched offering, a loaded

spoon, and instead fingered several pieces of pasta and brought them to her mouth. Afterward, she held out her hand to show me the residue of food still clinging to her fingers. My mind flashed back to when she helped feed my toddler. When my daughter dirtied her tiny fingers after exploring her meal, Mom would shake her head and say "sticky" and then wipe her hands clean. I did the same thing to my mom. I insisted that Mom take the spoon in her hands despite her effectiveness at getting food to her mouth. I'm just not ready to see her eat like a toddler yet.

Her eyes went from the spoon to the food and it was obvious that she was not calculating how to operate the spoon. It was a decision as to what she wanted in her hands the most. The food won. She dropped the spoon and reached for the pasta. I retrieved the spoon, loaded it and put it back in her hand.

There are four ways of inserting a spoon in your mouth, but only one way effectively delivers the food. The bowl of the spoon, the part containing the food, must be upright. Sipping the slender handle of the spoon as if it's a straw, does not accomplish the goal.

Purple lines marked her palm, likely from repeated attempts to replace the cap from a marker. As she brought the food to her mouth, she saw the colored ink, and she started chuckling. Then she turned her hand over to get a better look. The food from her spoon spilled in her lap. When her explanation of some random event required large expansive arm movements, her food was flung outward, creating new spots on the walls and carpet. Her aide told me it can take an hour to feed her. I understand now.

When she appeared bored with the pasta and okra, I stuck a fork in the dessert and delivered it to her mouth. (I decided it was safer if I took over the driving) Her eyes danced and her lips curved up with the first bite.

I'd been worried about the forced isolation to her room. Her world kept shrinking. From her home to the assisted living center apartment, a move to the smaller memory care unit and finally the confinement to a single room. It turned out that her imprisonment didn't really affect her as long as there was chocolate cake in a styrofoam cup.

∾

I'VE HEARD some potential wonderful news, but I have to give you some background first.

In 1901, Dr Aois Alzheimer's found Auguste, a 51-year-old housewife sitting on her hospital bed with a befuddled expression. When she died five years later, he performed an autopsy, slicing and staining her brain to see if he could explain her impaired memory and paranoia. He found extensive shrinking of her brain, neurofibrillary tangles and plaques, findings considered normal in a significantly *older* person. Something odd was happening.

For the next century, scientists continued to study the changes taking place in the brain of an Alzheimer's victim. Newer technologies: electron microscopes, MRI, and spect scanners, allowed closer inspection of the diseased organ. It's like examining the twisted, mangled frame of a car to discover what caused the wreck. Brake failure? Drunk driving? Engine malfunction? As the researchers bend over, thumping on tires and measuring engine oil, they can hear the screeching of brakes, the shattering of glass, the shrill sound of metal crumpling and tearing and they know another accident has occurred right around the corner. And then another. But they're not really accidents, are they?

Each neuron in our brain is connected to 7,000 other neurons. This is the cell most people remember from science class, the one that processes and sends signals along the

information superhighway of the brain. But it's another type of cell, the glial cell, that has become the focus of more research. If you watched *West Wing*, think of Leo McGarry, Josh, Toby and CJ as the glial cells for the president, Jed Bartlet. They arranged his meals, supported, and insulated him. The glial cells also, in a more apt comparison of Doug Stamper to Frank Underwood in *House of Cards*, destroy and remove any potential dangers to the neuron.

In Alzheimer's disease, Doug Stamper is failing at his job. Protein fragments called beta-amyloids create plaques that destroy the connections between the neurons (called synapses), impairing the ability to send messages to other parts of the brain. Neurofibrillary tangles, composed of tau proteins, prevent the transport of nutrition inside the cell. Doug failed to purge the threat and now, choked off externally and internally, the neuron cell begins to die. To make matters worse, instead of clearing the waste, the glial cells release chemical bombs in an attempt to destroy the evidence. And more neurons are killed.

But what happened to Doug in the first place? Why isn't he doing his job? The list of possibilities is long and varied and includes: hypertension, Down's syndrome, disordered sleep, high blood sugar, genetic mutations, head injury, obesity and even a bacteria found in gum disease. Doug Stamper was an alcoholic, that's on the list too. I watch my blood pressure, exercise, and floss regularly, but until they come up with something definitive, I'm not stopping the chocolate.

Since Grandpa died in 1990, I've watched the ticker tape of drug studies on Alzheimer's. The average study takes twelve to eighteen years and costs billions of dollars. Current drugs (as I write this book) may slow the decline, but there's been no drug that has prevented or halted the progression of the disease. Thirty years of losing money has meant fewer

companies are interested in continuing their research. It has been disheartening to watch.

Which brings me to an article I read about recently. Mice with brain findings similar to Alzheimer's were exposed to strobe lights and pulsing sounds. Practically a rodent rave party, right? The stimulation caused a reaction in their glial cells. Now, I'm not saying the glial cells waltzed, but they did start doing their job. They cleared the waste and the memory problems reversed. *Reversed*. Human studies are underway, and I'm dancing about the news.

~

THE RESIDENTS LOOKED like dressed mannequins sitting quietly around their tables as they waited for lunch. Mom was in a great mood. I pulled up a chair and found that she was engaged in a conversation with a newcomer to her left. It didn't take long before she grew frustrated by mom's nonsensical chatter.

The woman across from us looked like she recovering from a wild night of partying. She wore a sweater over her pajamas and her hair, a mixture of brown and grey strands, was uncombed. I imagined she missed breakfast because she swiveled in her chair, watching the servers distribute the meals.

The Diva unofficially joined our table. She pulled a chair to the corner and leaned forward as if confiding a secret. I admired her jeweled brooch as she explained how one of the gentleman had just had all of his teeth removed. "He's feeling much better," she hastened to reassure the table. The news had no effect on Mom, she bounced in her chair in rhythm to the music: "Yakety Yak" by the Coasters and "Hit the Road Jack" by Ray Charles. It was like sitting next to a toddler, bounding with energy.

Having delivered her news, the Diva stood up and looked around to see where she could spread her gossip. A server intercepted her and handed her a plate with a hot dog and chips. The Diva took a moment to examine the lunch offerings and found them unacceptable. She pushed the plate to the center of the table and, forgetting her task of spreading news about the toothless man, resumed her seat.

The hungry woman across from Mom snatched the hot dog out of its bun. Holding it with two hands, she nibbled at it like it was corn on the cob. Once it disappeared, she gripped a spoon in her right hand and a fork in her left. She held them upright in tightly fisted hands and stared straight ahead. Still hungry looking.

Mom shimmied her shoulders when "Pretty Woman" started playing. Then she lifted the black napkin from her lap and placed it on her head like a veil. The Diva saw the resemblance, pointed to Mom, and exclaimed, "Mary, Mother of God!"

Mom bolted up and pivoted in a circle, searching for the woman she's been praying to for her entire life. Her expression became despondent when she failed to spot the Holy Mother, and then she dropped dejectedly back down in her chair. I pulled the napkin from her head and replaced it in her lap. By the time the song changed, her mood lifted again.

One of our table mates took a bite of her pureed food and started coughing and choking. Tears came to her eyes, and she flapped her hands as if trying to take flight. Not to be outdone, the Diva flung her hand forward to show off her newly painted ruby-colored nails. The manicure was lovely, and no one required resuscitation.

At the table beside us, the server offered an option of churros (a fried dough dessert) or pumpkin pie. Churros is not a term known to everyone, but everyone knows what Cherrios are. "Cheerios!" came the response. The server tried

to explain, but it was too late. The entire table was demanding the same thing. "Cheerios! Cheerios!"

I could hear them discussing the uprising at the prep station. "We can make that happen. We can get those Cheerios if we need to."

Mom waved her napkin to the beat of the new song, "Lollipop". Her neighbor may not understand what Mom was saying, but she liked the show. She winked at Mom and tapped her foot under the table.

The Captain's wife was at a far side of the room and for a moment I was sad for her. It's not until I looked closer at her table companions that I recognized the man himself. He was incognito, wearing glasses I'd not seen before, and he'd switched his knitted stocking cap for a khaki fishing hat. I'm thrilled to see him and when he caught me staring, I gave him a thumbs-up similar to his own classic signal. He thumped his fist on the table in tune with the music and then flashed a toothless smile.

The servers swung their hips and did some twirls when "Hit the Road, Jack" came on, but wasn't until "Respect" by Aretha Franklin played that the party really got rolling. One of the male servers standing at the prep station used a metal spatula to bang out the rhythm. Another server used a tablespoon as a microphone, singing into it as she worked the crowd—she nodded her head, shook her hips and lip-synced the words. When she held the spoon-mic up to one of the lady residents, the grey-haired woman shouted out R-E-S-P-E-C-T!

I scanned the room. Some residents were grinning and enjoying the show. Others, like Mr. Complacent, were oblivious. (He spent the lunch hour trying to figure out how the silverware fit together.) The noise didn't bother Sleeping Beauty, she leaned precariously over her plate in a full snore. A few of the residents looked disgruntled, irritated by the

noise and boisterous servers. But Mom—Mom was grinning, eyes shining, as she danced in her chair.

And, for one shimmering moment, I believed everything would turn out all right.

∽

I HAD a text from my sister. Mom had an unpleasant episode, and "they want to meet with us." This provoked the same anxiety as *you need to report to the principal's office* or *the boss wants a word with you.* She's bitten three aides in the last week, broken the skin twice.

I had a restless night, unsure of what direction they would take. Would they ask her to leave?

*I should start investigating other memory centers nearby.*

Would they insist her medicines be adjusted?

*I can work with that. It could be tricky, though. The sedation designed to decrease the aggression, could cause more falls.*

Would they be open to looking at why this was happening? The episodes are not daily. The potential list that I'd drawn up in my head to explain her actions was: urinary tract infection (they've already tried and failed to get urine), constipation, toothache, loud noises, new aides not 'reading her signals" and finally—and most consistently—lack of sleep.

Our discussion was careful and measured on both ends of the table. All participants nodded their heads in agreement over possible causes. They wanted us to consider a new medical provider who specialized in psychiatric care, and we filled out the forms. There was a comment about transferring Mom if the situation did not improve. Afterward, my sister asked, "Did that sound like a threat to you, too?"

I can't imagine they'd bluff about this. I don't blame them,

I just hoped we could make it stop. After thanking us for making time to meet with them, I entered the memory care.

Mom was having a heated conversation with someone eating scrambled eggs. The diner appeared oblivious to Mom's tirade. Mom's nightgown was unbuttoned, revealing a mid-century modern crucifix and more than a little of her décolletage. Her feet were bare, she was shivering, and she had that wild-eyed look that meant we were in big trouble. I took her to her room before the situation escalated.

Clothing vomited out of her dresser drawers, one slipper accessorized the window sill and hangers, still loaded with her clothing, fanned out in front of the closet. She'd tugged the sheets from her bed, but thoughtfully placed her stuffed puppy in the middle of her pillow. A trail of toilet paper led to the bathroom where smears of toothpaste painted the countertop.

There was a time when I would have rushed to restore the room to its original order. A time when I believed I could harness the bedlam of the situation. I can't. But I'm getting better at floating on top of the current. Instead of cleaning up the room, I pushed the button on the CD player. Dionne Warwick's "Do You Know the Way to San Jose" is powerful vocal magic. Mom stopped her pacing and stared at the speaker.

*Maybe...*

I wrapped my arms around her body and felt her stiffen in response. She didn't shove me away, but her glare was still scorching. I leaned my head forward, whispered the words of the song in her ear.

*Maybe...*

I'd glued our bodies together with my hug so when I started swaying my hips, she was forced to start moving too. At first we just shuffled back and forth; I could sense she was

listening to the lyrics when she'd closed her eyes. I thought I heard a humming from her lips.

*I've got you now.*

She maneuvered herself out of my arms and her movements became more expansive. Her arms swept sideways, her body followed. She nodded her head in tune with the rhythm, leisurely spun in a circle when she felt the urge, and then clapped her hands at the end of the song.

I clicked the replay button.

## EPILOGUE

*Do not be frightened friend, Let us dance our way to God.*
— Kamand Kajouri

There is no ending to this story. My mother will die of Alzheimer's just as my grandfather did, and her death will not provide any conclusions. It's a song that never ends. As she's delivered from the suffering of her disease, the fear and reality of this illness will strike my generation. The odds are strong that at least one of my sisters, or myself, will be next in line.

Elisabeth Kübler-Ross described the steps to grieving—denial, anger, bargaining, defeat and acceptance. I went through them all with mom's diagnosis. I wonder whether you have to start over if the heavy mantle of the disease falls on you? Perhaps. I don't have any real answers.

I waited for the God of the Old Testament to repair the situation when mom was diagnosed with Alzheimer's. My mom was his servant her entire life—she'd attended church

regularly and surrounded all of us in prayer. I counted on God to spread the sea and let Mom cross safely. Instead, the God of the New Testament showed up, the one that allowed his own Son to die on the cross. And just as it took me years to understand the reasoning, the depth, and the impact of that sacrifice, I'm sure it will take years to grasp the necessity of my mother walking this path. I'm not there yet.

On to anger. I see injustice all around me daily. Children starving around the world. Women raped and receiving no help. I used to think every situation had a remedy. Every problem a solution. Alzheimer's is like a mudslide, gaining momentum and wiping out everything in its path before you can figure out how to divert it. It's a betrayal of everything I'd believed in. I spent a lot of time in this stage, although I might have described it in other terms. Frustration. Righteous outrage. I'd like to say I'm still angry, that I can still rally to fight, but the truth is, I'm tired. And one fights with more strength when one believes victory is possible.

I promised myself that I'd give Mom a soft landing—that's what I called it. In exchange for reducing my hours at work and devoting my spare time to be with her—she would walk this path gracefully and painlessly. Ouch. I was bargaining with a salesman who'd never seen the product. Years ago, I was trying to check out library books with my toddler son and with one swipe, he upended the contents of my purse onto the counter in front of the librarian. Scattered between us lay my lipstick, tampons, several wadded up tissues, a half-eaten cookie and a spare pacifier. The librarian took one look at the mess and then shook her head. "There's no dignity in motherhood." There's no dignity in Alzheimer's either. No modesty, no personal space, no propriety. Alzheimer's strips you bare and then picks at the bones left behind. There is no protecting a victim, no shielding them from what's ahead.

The defeat doesn't come in a single moment of insight. It's insidious. It's a stacking of failures, a realization that although you knew there was no cure—you discover that you can't always provide comfort either. It robs you of the ability to meet societal expectations, and leaves you struggling to provide basic human necessities—food, warmth, sleep—for the one you love.

What does acceptance look like? It's a gift that arrives in a dozen small packages. When I waved a toothbrush in front of Mom's mouth and she backed away with terror-stricken eyes, I put my weapon down and gave her a hug. When she could no longer cross an invisible line into the facility's small beauty shop, I braided her hair as she giggled. When she pressed her lips closed against green vegetables, I spoon-fed her chocolate cake. I shrugged my shoulders when she wouldn't let me clean the smear of food off her chin, ignored the appearance of clothing and bedding labeled with another resident's name, and conceded that hiding her medication in white powdered donuts is a brilliant idea. Lastly, and most importantly, *I learned to dance.*

# RESOURCES AND
# RECOMMENDATIONS

There is a growing list of resources available to help families dealing with this disease—I've listed only a *few*. I'd be cautious about reading the newest Alzheimer's research. I did this for years, and it's a bit like playing Whack-a-Mole. I keep getting my hopes up, but the beast gets away every time.

Alzheimer's Association- alz.org

A great resource for general information, but also explores more in-depth topics including current research. Local resources, professionals and support, can be searched in this site.

The Woman's Alzheimer's Movement- https://thewomensalzheimersmovement.org/

A non-profit, founded by Maria Shriver, dedicated to raising awareness about a woman's risk for Alzheimer's. They raise money to fund research and move us closer to a cure. I follow Maria on Instagram too. The posts are uplifting and remind me to take a deep breath when I'm stressed out.

Hilarity for Charity- https://wearehfc.org/

A non-profit led by Seth Rogen and Lauren Miller Rogen. Their mission is to care for families with this disease and educate young people about living a brain-healthy life. Seth's stand-up comedy to raise awareness about Alzheimer's can be found on Netflix.

## AFTERWORD

Do not be misled into believing that I am alone in supporting and caring for my mother. The burden of Alzheimer's is too heavy for one person.

My family (my husband, children, sisters, uncle, nieces, and nephews) circle around Mom, and each contribute their time, energy and love. If they wrote their own book, the stories would read differently, but the conclusion would be the same.

We are blessed to have each other.

**If you have a moment, could you write a review of this book?** Perhaps include how you've been able to stay connected to your loved one? We need to share our stories more!

# ABOUT THE AUTHOR

Susan Badaracco is the author of contemporary young adult fantasy books. She draws on past experiences, mythology and travel to spin tales of high-stakes adventure that explore the bonds of friendships and family.

When not writing she can be found taking a walk, cooking with home-grown herbs, or curled up in a chair with a book or two.

This is her first non-YA book. You can read more about her on her website:

Susanbadaracco.com

BLANK PAGE

BLANK PAGE